THE DRIFTING
Marriage

THE DRIFTING

Marriage

DONALD R. HARVEY Ph.D.

FLEMING H. REVELL COMPANY
OLD TAPPAN, NEW JERSEY

Harvey, Donald R. (Donald Reid).
  Drifting marriage.
  1. Marriage—Religious aspects—Christianity.
I. Title.
BV835.H37 1988   248.8'4   87-28460
ISBN 0-8007-1571-3

Copyright © 1988 by Donald R. Harvey
Published by the Fleming H. Revell Company
Old Tappan, New Jersey 07675
Printed in the United States of America

CONTENTS

FOREWORD
By Pat and Jill
Williams

For two and a half years, the frantic phone calls and heartbreaking letters have poured into our home. It seems every day brings another sad story about a marriage that has collapsed or is drifting to the same conclusion. The real tragedy is that too many of these hurting marriages involve Christians. And like the Pat and Jill Williams of several years ago, many of these people seem as if they "have it all together." But it's all an act, and in most cases, even their closest friends do not know that real problems lurk underneath.

We are not professionally trained conselors, but we are insatiable readers. In fact, we have read just about every book published on building great marriages and families.

As we share with people, individually, in couples, or in larger groups, we have been recommending two books. *Rekindled* (Revell) is the story of our own troubled marriage. It offers not only what led us to a confrontation but also the specific and practical steps we took to ignite our marriage again. More important, it gives the hope and encouragement that if two people will commit themselves to working at their marriage, it can be the best, as God originally intended.

Love Life for Every Married Couple (Zondervan) by Dr. Ed Wheat is the textbook for taking God's marriage principles and applying them to the marital relationship. Many ministers and seminary professors have written or called us to say that these two books have been and will continue to be on the required reading list for every engaged couple and potential minister.

From now on we will be strongly recommending a third book. *Drifting Marriage* is an answer to prayer for Christian marriages headed toward disaster. Dr. Donald Harvey has had years of experience studying and working with troubled marriages, and he shares powerful information that is desperately needed.

We measure the quality of a book by the amount of marking and underlining we do. By the time we reached the last chapter of *Drifting Marriage*, almost every page had been marked.

You will find this the most helpful material ever written on the causes of drfting marriages, detailing many different contributors to the problem. More important, you will discover practical measures to use in correcting the problems and building a strong marriage. Read with pen in hand because you are certain to be saddened, convicted, stimulated, and encouraged to work harder to change many aspects of your own marriage.

The number-one enemy of Christian marriage is the subtle drifting away from each other. We must fight this problem in our own marriage every day, because we never get to the point of perfection. The natural inclination to drift never disappears.

Dr. Harvey concludes that "God has a future . . . and a future with God is always good." We all have a bright future to look forward to with God as the head of our marriages, and we are positive that our own home will be stronger as a result of studying Dr. Harvey's marvelous book.

PAT AND JILL WILLIAMS

PART ONE

THE PROBLEM OF DRIFTING

— 1 —
DRIFTING:
THE
DANGER

Drifting is one of the most common forms of marital failure. In fact, I would venture to say that the majority of those couples found in our churches from Sunday to Sunday have marriages which are "adrift." Just think about that for a moment. Look across the pews. Would you guess that a majority of your friends have marriages that are in trouble? Probably not. Neither would they.

Drifting. Not only is it the most common form of marital failure, it is also the most dangerous. It is subtle. It is quiet. It is non-offensive. It sounds no alarms. It just gradually creeps into our lives. And then it destroys.

Step by step, the emotional deadness sneaks up on us as we move further and further away from our mates. The appearance of "all is well" is our placard. We fail to see the absence of real caring. Why should we see it? We have our preoccupations to keep us busy. The absence of emotional pain is accepted as a sign that everything is okay. We are busy, we are content, and everything is "fine." We have grown accustomed to the way things are.

As it was with Adam in the garden thousands of years ago, Christians today are seldom troubled with problems of the obvious. Whether it be our personal life or our marital relationship, seldom is it the blatant, the obvious, the visibly immoral which presents us with the most difficulty. Wrangling . . . viciousness . . . open combativeness . . . these are not the characteristics of the failing

11

Christian marriage. We have a far more subtle form of failure—we drift.

I am reminded of Paul's observation to Timothy:

> While there are people whose offences are so obvious that they run before them into court, there are others whose offences have not yet overtaken them.
>
> 1 Timothy 5:24

I am afraid that, for many Christian marriages "whose offences have not yet overtaken them," it is only a matter of time.

Drifting marriages are affairs waiting to happen. Such was the case with Susan and Terry. Married sixteen years, who would have thought that Terry would have an affair. They seemed like an ideal couple. Having similar backgrounds and values, they met in a denominational college. Their two-year courtship was wonderful and they married immediately upon graduating. Both Susan and Terry enjoyed careers and, somehow in their busy schedules, managed to have a family and to be actively involved in their church. Terry's employment as principal of a Christian school and part-time director of music in his church had him even more integrally involved in positions of ministry than most laymen. They seemed to be an all-American family. At least, this was the way it appeared until Terry left Susan to live with another woman.

I really don't know what happened. I was totally surprised when Terry left. I know some women seem to have some clues that their husbands are being unfaithful. But I didn't have the slightest hint.

What was even more surprising was the degree of dissatisfaction Terry said he had been experiencing. I thought things were fine. But he said he'd been unhappy for years. I asked why he didn't say anything about it earlier so we could work on it. All he said was that he didn't realize how unhappy he was until he met Doris. And then, he said, it was too late to work on anything.

Theoretically, marriages of this kind can drift along indefinitely . . . and some do. As long as nothing significant occurs to create a change in the routine, the failing nature of these relationships may never become apparent. However, given the right set of circumstances, a chain reaction of events can completely destroy the fragile shell of this type of marriage. This was the fate of Susan and Terry.

I would not want you to believe that the precipitants which create the marital crisis are narrowly focused on extramarital involvements . . . the "affairs." There are other disrupters equally effective at bringing the failing nature of drifting marriages to the surface. For example, the outside involvement does not have to be a full-blown affair for its effects to be made known. It may be only a passing emotional encounter. At least, this was what occurred with Dave and Chris.

Dave and Chris married when they graduated from high school. After two years of marriage they began attending a local church, were converted, and became instrumentally involved in many of its functions. They were pillars . . . the kind of couple a pastor points to with pride.

Like most of us, Dave and Chris had their own personal peculiarities. For Chris, it was a tendency to be very direct . . . almost too direct at times. She had a sharp tongue. Dave, on the other hand, was an extremely easygoing sort of person . . . an all-around nice guy. He didn't like conflict and when Chris would get "direct" with him, he tended to avoid any form of confrontation.

As time passed, Dave found it easier to avoid the home front. This lessened his chances of being involved in any tense situations with Chris. With church programs and his job, staying away from home was easy. Chris adjusted to Dave's distancing by returning to school. She worked on her college degree and, once it was completed, began a career. Although never verbalized, they had negotiated a tolerable existence . . . they had achieved a comfortable distance from one another. In short, they had drifted.

This comfortable arrangement could probably have continued for years—had it not been for Janet. Dave and Chris had not planned on Janet.

Janet and her husband started attending their church. In fact, Dave was their Sunday-school teacher. As a part of fellowship responsibilities, the two couples began to interact socially. They got together after church, went out to dinner, and even spent some time together recreationally on the weekend. There seemed to be a natural fit for the two couples as they developed a friendship. Unfortunately, however, the "friendship" between Dave and Janet grew far beyond the bounds of what it needed to be. It became very romantic in nature.

Janet, like Dave, was very distant from her mate. Dave's easygoing nature was very appealing to her. So they began to meet privately to discuss their respective marital disappointments and dissatisfactions. After a brief period of time, they both realized what was happening. Although they had not been sexually active, they both saw the real potential for that to occur. They were extremely emotionally involved. Rather than risk the possibility of their relationship proceeding any further and destroying two families, Janet and Dave decided to stop meeting.

Shortly after this decision, employment opportunities required Janet and her husband to move to another city. You would have thought that this would have totally solved Dave's problem. But it didn't. He became moody and grouchy. He was no longer the easygoing husband that Chris had lived with for 15 years. Finally, Chris confronted him about the change in his behavior and he responded by telling her everything. In shock, Chris contacted me for an appointment.

What was most significant about meeting with this couple during our first session was Dave's insight into what had happened.

> You know, I'm no longer interested in Janet. I was when we decided to call it off. That was difficult to do. But we both knew it wouldn't have worked anyway.
>
> After a while, though, I didn't feel any more pain where Janet was concerned. She kind of breezed into my life and then breezed out. She's no longer a problem for Chris and me. What is a problem, however, is the emptiness that is in our marriage.
>
> I didn't really know the emptiness was there until I met Janet. Wow, I really felt something for her. But after she left, I realized how little there actually was between Chris and me. There was just this big empty hole where a relationship used to be.
>
> I can't stand the emptiness. I've got to have something more. And if I can't get it here, I'll probably get out of the marriage.

Although short in duration, Dave's contact with Janet was significant enough to rekindle previously dormant emotions. Once these senses were revitalized, he found it impossible to return to a mundane, unemotional life. The realization of the emotional emptiness in his relationship with Chris forced a crisis in his marriage . . . a crisis that had to be resolved. It was not the marriage that had changed. It had been the same for years . . . dead. But this brief encounter with Janet made Dave aware of what he was missing. He decided he didn't want to "go without" any longer.

Even though Dave had not been involved in an affair, the precipitant which prompted his marital crisis was still a third person. In reality, however, many of the precipitants to marital crises have nothing to do with third parties or romantic "significant others." All that really has to happen for a crisis to occur is for the failing nature of the marriage to be made known. The pensive self-evaluation which often accompanies the mid-life crisis; the disruption brought about by the departure of children as they reach maturity; a geographical relocation which causes a mate to lose previous preoccupations; a close friend who has an affair or gets a divorce; the list is extensive. Any one of these is powerful enough to disrupt a drifting marriage which previously appeared both calm and stable. Remember, anything that brings awareness of the failing nature of the marriage is a potential disrupter.

Lately, I have been working a great deal with marital separation. If I have learned anything at all in dealing with these relationships that are on the verge of breaking up, it is this: no one leaves a healthy marriage. You may leave to be with someone else. These are the affairs. You may leave out of frustration. This is when you become aware of the deadness in the marriage and choose to leave rather than working on restoration. Or, you may leave at the encouragement of your mate. This is sometimes the case when repeated irresponsibility abounds. But no one leaves a healthy, happy marriage. No one has yet reported "marital satisfaction" as the reason for their separation.

The point is this: Drifting marriages are never satisfying relationships. The mates are never happy. They may be tolerant. They may be complacent. They may even be minimally content. But they are not happy. Their marriage is anemic. It is dull . . . mundane . . . it lacks life, vitality, and vibrancy. The boundaries around healthy marriages are more than strong enough to deal with the circumstances mentioned above. The potential third parties, the mid-life crises, the departure of children . . . these are adequately handled by marriages that are emotionally alive. But in drifting marriages, mates find little to hold them together and are susceptible to many forms of disruption. Due to this failing nature, their destruction is predictable.

Couples who are drifting seldom come for counseling, at least while the marriage is still intact. They are too content to let things just go on as they are. If seen at all, it is usually in the aftermath. A wife will come to me asking for help in coping with the departure of her husband. "I can't sleep; I can't eat; I can't manage." A husband will call asking advice as to how he can regain the forsaken affections of his wife. How can the inclination, the spark of former years, be regained? Amazing as it may seem, even in these lifeless relationships, there can be an immense emotional response to the loss of a mate. Rejection is difficult to tolerate, regardless of the circumstances.

Yet it is often too late. Emotional pulls are powerful, often overruling what we may have previously believed to be the right thing to do. We seem to have difficulty with the notion of influence and emotions. People in general, and specifically those within the conservative church community, fail to have a healthy respect for the power of the human emotional system. We prefer to view mankind as being totally rational and fully capable of easily doing the "right" thing. We like to think that telling a man what he "should," "ought," or "must" do is all that is necessary. I am afraid we tend to have our "heads in the sand." The influence of emotions is powerful. And failing to respect this power is dangerous. This is not to legitimize its influence . . . only to acknowledge it.

Our tendency to deny the powerful influence of emotions can be illustrated with the case of Larry and Diana. This couple had been married for thirteen years when Diana scheduled a counseling appointment. Larry did not attend the session. What unfolded was a story with which I have become far too familiar.

Larry and Diana had been another "ideal couple." He was a university professor and she was a homemaker and mother. They were active in their church and community and, from Diana's account, had the typical American marriage. They were busy, but other than that, she had no complaints. She did not think Larry had any either, at least until he decided to leave.

One day, Larry came home, packed his bags, and announced that he was leaving. He didn't know whether he wanted a divorce or not. All that he knew was that he was tired of the rut he had gotten into. "I'm tired of everything being so dull."

Diana was shocked. She pleaded with Larry to reconsider. He didn't. He would not go to counseling, nor would he wait. He had to get out. He couldn't breathe in the house. He needed some space. Larry told Diana that there was no other woman in his life. He had just realized how frustrated he was with everything and he needed some time to think. So he was leaving.

What seemed to shock Diana the most, in addition to Larry's abrupt departure, was his total reversal in behavior. He had been so responsible throughout the marriage . . . the perfect husband. I asked her what she thought had happened.

I'm not sure. But I think he's possessed. Satan's got a hold of him. What else would explain his total reversal in behavior? Maybe he's on drugs. There's a lot of that at the university. Maybe his mind just snapped. He has been under a lot of pressure lately. It's got to be one of these. How else could you explain his sudden crazy behavior?

How else, indeed? How we tend to deny the power of the emotions! Again, this is not to legitimize or to give license to our emotional systems. But it is imperative that we recognize the influence which emotions, if not dealt with appropriately, can have on our lives.

As the case of Larry and Diana illustrates, it is this power of emotions which creates the difficulty with allowing marriages to drift. If allowed to drift until interrupted by a crisis, the emotions are so strong that any hope for intervention is almost too late. Diana thought Larry was either being possessed by Satan, under the influence of drugs, or possibly having some unknown mental disturbance. What else could explain his crazy behavior? What else, indeed? Diana simply failed to appreciate the power of our emotions.

When the disrupter is something that draws attention to the deadness of the relationship, the frustration of feeling trapped in a lifeless form often **pushes** a mate out of the marriage. When the particular disrupter is a third party, the fresh and pulsating emotions **pull** a mate out of the dry, lifeless marriage. Regardless of the motivation, whether *pulled* out or *pushed* out, the "want to" for the marriage seems to be gone. And without the "want to," it is difficult for any individual to move back toward a mate who has been an emotional stranger for years. This is the fate of those who drift. This is the danger. And it is a danger to be feared.

Prevention and Change

When a marriage fails, who is at fault? When a crisis finally occurs in a drifting relationship, who do we blame? Both mates? Neither mate? In an affair, is it the person breaking up the couple?

It is neither easy nor necessary to determine who is at fault . . . whom we can blame. Much more constructive use of our energies can be made in determining what can be done to change these relationships prior to the point of crisis. Or better yet, what can be done to prevent them from ever occurring. How do we stop marriages from drifting?

As you can see, the destructive nature of drifting is my *concern*. As a result of this concern, my *intent* is to somehow reduce the stranglehold which this failing scenario has on so many of our marriages. How can the grip be lessened?

I believe that the answer to effective intervention in any form of marital failure rests with two key elements: recognition and responsibility.

Recognition

Before you can constructively try to change, you must first recognize what is happening. Some couples seemingly exist for years with little insight or awareness of the failing condition of their marriages. Failing to recognize the problem, they just "roll on" indefinitely. A primary goal in prevention, therefore, is to clarify what is happening . . . to identify how we drift.

Responsibility

As essential as recognition may be, however, it is even more important that you be willing to accept personal responsibility for changing the relationship. You must "do" something. Ultimately, the responsibility for change always rests with the couple. Unless you are willing to make some active efforts to change what is happening, there is very little chance that your relationship will be improved. A second goal in prevention, therefore, is to take responsibility for your marriage and to behave differently.

If applied to your marriage, I believe that the material offered in this book can help prevent the drifting form of marital failure from ever occurring. For some, this material will have more of a restorative effect because you are already drifting. For others, it will be an opportunity to avoid embarking upon the drifting road to destruction.

Regardless of your present marital condition, and whether your need is preventative or restorative, it is not too late to build a happy marriage. It takes only recognition and a willingness to try.

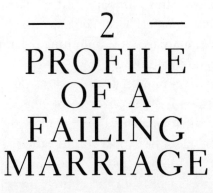

— 2 —
PROFILE
OF A
FAILING
MARRIAGE

It was unusual for me to see a couple like John and Linda in my marriage counseling practice. What was so unusual about them was that they were not in crisis. No one was threatening to leave. No one was filing for divorce. In fact, no one was even mad. Then why would they even come for counseling? John summed up the reason this way:

> Linda and I have been married for fifteen years. We have three lovely children, a house, two cars, a dog, and a cat. I guess you'd say we have everything we're supposed to have. We don't argue. In fact, we work very well together. We even like each other. But we don't know if we love each other. At least, we know we don't to the extent that we once did.

> We don't know what happened. I know I've been real involved in building my business. And with three kids, it's easy to figure out what Linda's been doing. But now we're concerned with where the marriage is going. Neither one of us wants out. But we're afraid that if we don't do something to change what's happening—who knows where it will go?

Linda and John were lucky. They saw that something was wrong, and they were able to do something about it before it became too late. Recognizing what was happening, they made some changes. Others are not always this fortunate. In fact, it was the divorce of some close friends, another "ideal couple," which caused them to evaluate their own marriage. It is unfortunate that their friends did not have the same opportunity.

We live in a time of unprecedented marital disruption. Never in our nation's history has the divorce rate been as high or the occurrence of extramarital affairs as prevalent. Sadly, in the midst of the chaos, Christendom has not been unscathed. Those within the Church are also contributing to these growing statistics.

The pastor who ran off with the church organist; the Sunday-school teacher who had an affair with her neighbor; the layman who divorced his wife to marry his secretary; all figurative examples with which, unfortunately, we are all familiar. It is a rare church which has been untouched by such happenings.

A simplistic response would be to say that those who become involved in these types of extramarital relationships are either emotionally unstable or suffering from extreme personality defects. In reality, however, we know that this is not the case. Granted, there are instances where this is truer than not, but this is more the exception than the rule. It is far more typical for us to find that those in our congregations who become involved in relationships outside of their own marriages are actually ordinary people . . . much like John and Linda . . . much like you and me.

For the most part, these affairs happen accidentally. At least, they are unintentional as opposed to premeditated. The hypothetical pastor did not enter the relationship with the church organist intending to become emotionally involved to the point where he would eventually leave his wife. The disruption of his marriage was not planned. Regardless of his intentions, however, the results are the same . . . two devastated families.

A sad bit of irony accompanying this form of marital failure is that even though these affairs are largely accidental, given the circumstances, they are extremely predictable. They really come as no surprise if you know what to look for. What makes these situations so predictable are the marriages which spawn them . . . these marriages are *drifting*.

Drifting: A Description

The usual scenario for a drifting marriage starts innocently enough. In fact, it's almost typical. In the beginning, there are two mates who marry for "all the right reasons." They are in love and they have similar goals and values. They both seem to know what they want in life. They both have great expectations for the marriage.

Marriage is seen as a positive and not a negative. It is not viewed as a giving up of personal freedom but instead as an expansion. It is a new dimension . . . a completion . . . a fulfillment. The marriage begins with excitement. With many dreams riding on this joint venture, the typical couple anticipates a long and happy life together.

But we live in a demanding world. As housekeeping is established, the reality of just how demanding the world can be begins to set in. Neither husband nor wife is by nature an idle person. Each strives to achieve . . . to accomplish. Whether in the home or at the office, each wants to be good at what he does. Slowly, the "stress for success" element, so prevalent in our society, begins to eat away at the once-held marital priority. With this change in focus, the happy newlyweds begin to drift—not by design . . . not by desire . . . but by default.

Husbands who begin to drift exchange one preoccupation for another. Instead of focusing on the emotional and companionship needs of their wives, they become preoccupied with activities outside of the marriage. Although there are many pursuits strong enough to capture the interest of drifting husbands, the most common is business or career. With this particular preoccupation, it is easy to even justify the change in focus. "I'm working hard for my family . . . I need to provide for their security." Pastors and other religious husbands can be doubly pious when doing church work. They're "working for the Lord," and who can fault that kind of preoccupation? So with a strong feeling of justification, these overly preoccupied husbands throw themselves with righteous abandon into whatever it is that has such control over their lives.

The wives in drifting marriages have their own set of preoccupations. The most predominant is "the children," a natural preoccupation. In fact, you may even wonder how it can ever be avoided, especially when the children are younger and meeting their needs for nurturing and caretaking is, to say the least, demanding.

My wife, Jan, and I are parents. Trying to deal with the legitimate demands of the world we live in and still keep our relationship with one another as a high priority has prompted us to recognize the impact of children on a marriage. Our children have brought much joy to our lives. Yet, they have also required our attention—and lots of it. As with any of life's preoccupations, my concern is not with the children's legitimate demands for attention but with where the priority of the marital relationship is placed as we go about performing our parental responsibilities. As difficult as it may appear, there needs to be a balance. Mates have dual roles. They are parents . . . but they are also lovers. As the case of Linda and John illustrates, sometimes this balance is not achieved and the marriage drifts.

Some of the mothers in drifting marriages actually become so involved in the lives of their children as to interfere with their children's personal development. Not having a marital relationship to invest in, they direct all of their emotional energy toward the lives of their children. Overprotecting, sheltering, pampering . . . these well-intended characteristics are a detriment to parenting, not an asset. By the time these children reach adolescence, the consequence of this form of overinvolvement is usually inescapable. But even when drifting wives manage to avoid the extreme excessiveness of the pampering pitfall, it is only a matter of time before the unsuitability of this preoccupation catches up with them in another form. The children grow up. They leave home. Mom is out of a job. We now refer to this as the "empty nest syndrome." Where is she to invest her energies?

Obviously, in our modern society, there are interests other than children which can serve as preoccupations. Even though women are much more career oriented today than they have been in the past and there are ample opportunities for volunteer and/or church work, the pull toward the children still seems to be the most natural preoccupation for drifting wives.

Am I saying that careers aren't important? That we shouldn't be concerned about our children? That church work is passé? No, not at all. In fact, we know that the healthiest marriages are those where the husbands and wives have their own interests referred to as "healthy preoccupations." There needs to be "his, hers, and theirs." Husbands need interests and outlets. Wives need interests and outlets. It's not good to put all of our "emotional eggs" into one basket, even if it is the marriage.

Yet, my concern is with priorities. If we can be involved in our careers and still maintain the priority of the marriage, we are doing well. If we can be involved in the lives of our children and still maintain the priority of the marriage, we are doing well. But I find few couples who seem to be able to do this. In fact, *most* are not. It's obvious that John and Linda were not able to maintain a healthy balance between their personal involvements and a mutual investment in their marriage. When marriage is replaced by another priority, regardless of the worthiness of the substitute, you begin to drift. And a drifting marriage is a failing marriage.

The failing nature of the drifting marriage is seldom apparent.

Everything looks fine. There is nothing in a couple's interactions with one another to suggest the slightest difficulty. They are cordial . . . even friendly. You will remember that John said that he and Linda did not argue. In fact, they worked very well together. That's not an unusual report for drifting marriages. The typical couple openly cooperates, has little apparent difficulty in managing the mundane affairs of everyday life, offers no resistance, no foot-dragging. Things may even appear somewhat dull—but at least a disruptive outward display of hostility does not have a place in their drifting relationship. What more could you ask for? These marriages are frequently—and mistakenly—viewed by outsiders as being "ideal."

The emotional tone of the relationship, however, is far from ideal. In fact, it is virtually dead. They exchange pleasantries easily enough but there is no emotional feeling to go with these behaviors. It's as though they have struck a bargain. "You treat me nice and I'll treat you nice." But frequently, the bargain is a secret. So secret in fact, that they don't even realize it themselves.

For couples who drift, there is little true emotionality in the relationship. Things are emotionless. Interestingly, however, when things are emotionally dead, there is the absence of both the positive *and* the negative. With the absence of emotion, there is little to make the drifters feel good toward one another. With emotional distance, there is also very little pain. There may have been pain in the earlier years of the marriage. In fact, as the process of emotional distancing first began to occur, there may have been quite a bit of it. But now, after ample time for adjustments, the present situation is at least minimally satisfactory. There is no anger. There is no strife. There is no hint of resentment fighting to surface within the relationship. Rather, there is only a great void where once there was emotion. The couple is now anesthetized to feelings. Coldness is the norm . . . it is the accepted . . . it is the expected . . . it is "settled for." And this is a drifting marriage.

Drifting marriages are neither planned nor desired. Yet couples often seem powerless to prevent or change their situations. For whatever reasons, they seem willing to allow the marriage to just drift along. For weeks, months, even years . . . little or no constructive effort is made to remedy the ailing relationship. Again, not by design . . . not by desire . . . but by default.

Motivations to Drift

Couples who drift can make their initial move toward emotional distance for a variety of reasons or motivations. Some of these motivations are intentional . . . others are not. Still, they drift just the same.

External Demands

One reason for drifting is the responding to the external demands of living. I have already alluded to this motivation. In fact, this particular motivation probably best represents the case of Linda and John. As you will see, it is the least intentional of the preoccupational motivations.

Sometimes the mere stresses of everyday life are so demanding and constant that weary mates simply fail to recognize the toll being taken on their relationship. Keeping up with the children, paying the bills, managing schedules . . . this is no easy accomplishment. Subtly, mates fail to recognize the distance that creeps between them. All of a sudden, they no longer have anything to say to each other. If there are no problems with the household or the children, communication does not take place. Unintentionally, they have "lost touch."

In this overstressed existence, home becomes a refuge . . . a haven from the storm . . . a place for relaxing and recharging. You collapse in front of the television hoping to regain enough energy to contend with a taxing tomorrow which is understandable, comprehendible, and even justifiable. The problem comes with the frequency in which this exhaustion and home-as-a-filling-station cycle of living seems to overtake us. As my wife has commented to me in the past, "Sometimes we are so caught up in the *relaxing* that we never *relate*."

Natural Bents

Some couples enter a drifting relationship as a result of natural "bents" or tendencies. For example, I have already mentioned the "stress for success" element in our society.

When Trudy came to my office it was without her husband of nine years. Steve had celebrated the entering of a new year with the announcement that he wanted a divorce. He called this his "New Year's resolution." Trudy was crushed.

Trudy believed that her being totally unaware of Steve's dissatisfaction was at least partially to blame for her emotional devastation.

> I was totally surprised. I had no idea he was this unhappy.
> I knew things seemed a little strained. But I thought that it
> was me that felt the tension and not Steve. He seemed to be
> as happy as ever up until January first.

I never got an opportunity to talk with Steve to ascertain exactly how long he had been dissatisfied or what exactly precipitated his announcement. In desperation, for several weeks Trudy had pleaded with Steve to return home before she first came to see me. He refused. Even though I coached her in a different tack of relating to him, it was to no avail. Ultimately, Steve sued for divorce and their marriage became another statistic.

Even though there were many questions left unanswered, I was able to gather enough information from Trudy to figure out what had contributed to the deterioration of their relationship.

Steve was a natural. He could do anything he set his mind to. Anything. He had all the ingredients for success. He was capable, confident, and he had drive . . . lots of drive.

Let me tell you how much drive Steve had. He had so much drive that it seemed as though I never saw him. I thought things would get better as he got toward the top of the corporate ladder. But they didn't. They only got worse. Steve had such a streak of competitiveness.

During the last few years, we never took a genuine vacation. The children and I just got included in some of his business trips. Steve would be involved in meetings all day and then spend some of his evenings with us. But that was more than we got at home.

Steve's boss told me that Steve had the potential to really go far in his field. I guess I can see more clearly now what he meant. Anyone who would put in the kind of hours that Steve did would have to have potential. One thing he knew how to do was to sacrifice for success. I'm afraid, at least in our situation, what got sacrificed was the marriage.

Being highly competitive, Steve adamantly wanted to achieve . . . to accomplish. While drive like this was good for his career, it was devastating to his marriage. Highly motivated to pursue his work, the marriage slipped into a lesser place of priority. Career gradually took precedence over relationship and the marriage began to drift.

Something happened to bring the failing nature of the relationship to Steve's awareness. It's not really important what happened. What is important is that one day Steve realized the emotional distance in his marriage. Although he had contributed to the problem, this seemed to make little difference to him. He was obsessed with the emotional void and when he saw the relationship for what it was, he decided to get out.

Steve represents one aspect of natural bents. Another example of this motivational preoccupation is a strong allegiance to other people. Maybe these other people are old friends. Hunting and fishing buddies can have quite an influence on a husband. Or it may be someone even closer. I frequently hear complaints regarding meddling extended family members. The most notorious seems to be the mothers (or mothers-in-law). But I do hear of strong allegiances to fathers as well. Although we like to see healthy family relationships, when people marry, they are forming a new family. This new family unit should take precedence over their former relationships.

Finally, a motivational pull may be toward strong personal interests—a wife who is too interested in a social club or a husband in sports recreation. "Golfing widows" are a reality and not merely a figment of our imagination. Spending all week at the office and every weekend on the golf course will cause a marriage to drift about as fast as anything else I know.

Legitimate Excuses

Some mates find outside preoccupations to be a legitimate excuse to avoid the "homestead." For one reason or another, home is not where they want to be. Obviously, this motivational category is somewhat more intentional than the others we have discussed.

The "whys" can vary. Possibly a husband has grown tired of his wife and is aware of it. Perhaps some old and unresolved hurts have caused walls and barriers to emerge between them. Maybe closeness is uncomfortable. Regardless of the specific motivation, outside preoccupations are intentionally utilized to maintain emotional distance.

This type of motivation for drifting is sometimes inaccurately confused with the proverbial workaholic. The true workaholic is driven by internal desire. He has a strong need to achieve. The husband who throws himself into his work in order to avoid his wife is not a genuine workaholic. The **behavior** may be the same. But the **motivation** is far different.

I have a friend who falls into this category. He appears to be a workaholic and regularly works an eighty-hour week. He runs programs, writes books, gets things done—always does too much. He is seldom at home in the evening. Dedicated? Well, I suppose he is. But not as much as most people think. In reality, he simply has no desire to be at home. So he legitimately avoids it. As he drifts away, his marriage drifts apart.

Default

Finally, some mates choose to drift by default. This variation represents more of a defense than it does an offense. It is a response . . . but never a desired first choice. It is best illustrated by the words of Louise.

> I could see what was happening. Roger was gradually drifting away. He had his job, he had his friends, he had his hobbies . . . what did he need with me?
>
> I talked to him about it a couple of times but it didn't seem to make much difference. He kept on "doing his thing." So I decided I might as well accept things the way they were. Nothing was going to change. Roger was going to be Roger. That realization made things easier.
>
> I began to join clubs and started a life of my own. Now, I have my friends and he has his. I have my interests and he has his. And I have my activities and he has his. I guess things are working out O.K.

What does a wife do when her husband blatantly decides that he wants to invest more energy outside of the marriage than he does within? One of the more common choices seems to be to respond in kind and this is what Louise did. She retaliated with a similar distancing move.

For Louise, the intentional decision to find other friends, interests, and activities was not a first choice. Neither was it a preferred choice. But it was a choice nevertheless. In a spirit of depletion, an emotionally abandoned wife like Louise finally resigns herself to settle for less.

What Are the Consequences?

An interesting postscript can be made in reference to these four categories of motivations. Whether outside preoccupations are (1) totally unintentional, (2) natural bents or desires, (3) active attempts (excuses) to maintain some distance from a mate, or (4) an unwanted but resigned response to a mate who is already preoccupied with things outside of the relationship, the results are the same: *a drifting marriage.*

Much of the remainder of this book will look specifically at the elements which contribute to our drifting. Before discussing these contributors, however, I believe it is important to look further at the failing nature of a drifting marriage.

— 3 —
THE
NATURE
OF
DRIFTING

When describing the drifting marriage in the last chapter, you will recall words like *dangerous, failing,* and *destructive.* Those are strong terms. They leave little doubt as to my feelings. That's good. I do not want you to have any confusion regarding my perspective. In fact, I would like for you to share it.

Drifting is a terrible condition for a marriage to be in. It represents failure. As your understanding of the failing nature of this scenario increases, I believe that your fear of it will also increase. And if you fear it, you may guard against it.

Our society tends to misconstrue exactly what failure really is. When it comes to marriage we look to divorce statistics in order to take our pulse. In actuality, however, divorce statistics are quite misleading. Believe it or not, these figures actually paint a picture that is rosier than true life. The state of marriage is really far worse. As alarming as these figures may be, divorce statistics tell us only how many marriages *have ended.* They do not tell us how many marriages *are failing!* And it is the number of marriages which are actually failing that tells the true story.

How many marriages really are failing? Skillfully substituting appearance for possession, how many failing relationships are masquerading as happy marriages? How many mere shells of a marriage are being disguised with smiles and cordiality? How many marriages are continuing to **just** exist? Self-perpetuating, nonnourishing, highly predictable . . . they will **just be.** In short, how many are merely drifting? Answers to these questions would provide us with a far truer picture of the status of marriage today. And knowing the answers, I'm scared.

It was never the Lord's design for marriages to fail . . . whether ended in divorce or maintained in a lifeless form. Yet they are. And the reason they are is that they drift.

In order to better understand the relationship between drifting and marital failure, we need to see more clearly why we marry in the first place. Why do we marry? Why are we attracted to others? What is it that compels us to stumble through a selection process, enter courtship, and eventually marry someone of the opposite sex?

By and large, people in our society marry to achieve intimacy. We may not understand it; we may not be able to verbalize it; we may not even realize it. But it is this natural and ordained desire to love and be loved by another human being that compels us to drop our typically protective shields in order to gradually draw closer and closer and closer . . . to another.

We marry for intimacy. This being the case, it is our inability to attain the intimacy which we so longingly desire that causes our marriages to fail. It's not the proverbial other woman. Neither is it the mid-life crisis. These precipitate a marital crisis but they do not cause a marriage to fail. For these precipitants to create a crisis, the marriage must already be failing. And if it is failing, it is because the couple failed to grow together intimately.

Marriages, in general, fail because of the inability to attain intimacy. They lack internal bonding or connectedness. And this is the very reason drifting is a failing condition.

Drifting and intimacy are contradictory terms. You cannot drift and be close at the same time. You can drift and live together. You can drift and be cooperative. You can even drift and be minimally content. But you cannot drift and be close. And without closeness, your marriage is a failure. To be intimate, and thus to have a successful marriage, you must put drifting aside.

Understanding Marital Intimacy

For many people, intimacy is automatically placed within a sexual context. To be intimate is to be sexual. If you are not sexually active, then you are not intimate. If you are sexually active, then you are intimate. As we shall see, this is far from the truth.

In recent years, numerous authors have successfully argued that intimacy has a multidimensional character. In other words, it is made up of many elements as opposed to merely one. Transcending the narrowly defined focus on sexuality, intimacy has been found to include closeness in numerous other areas within a relationship. In fact, the absence of closeness in these other areas brings some question as to whether you are truly intimate. Since the failure to achieve intimacy is the primary culprit for marital failure, I believe we need to become aware of exactly what the dimensions of marital intimacy are.

In addition to identifying seven dimensions of intimacy (we will identify only six), Dr. David Olson has developed a test for measuring the degree of intimacy which exists within relationships. In his work with couples, Dr. Olson has found the following dimensions significant in determining intimacy within relationships.

1. Emotional intimacy. When you are emotionally intimate, you "feel" close to one another. You feel emotionally supported and cared for by your mate. There is a sharing of hurts and joys and a sense that each of you is genuinely interested in the well-being of the other. Attentiveness and understanding seem to be characteristics of this dimension of intimacy.

2. Social intimacy. When you are socially intimate, you have many friends in common as opposed to socializing separately. This is not to say that you do not have some separate friendships. But "separate friendships" are not the totality of your socializing. Having time together with mutual friends is an important part of your shared activities.

3. Sexual intimacy. True sexual intimacy involves more than the mere performance of the sex act. In truly intimate marriages, sexual expression is an essential part of the relationship. It is a communication vehicle and not just a duty. If your relationship is sexually intimate, you are satisfied with your sex life. You are comfortable with one another and do not see your activity as routine. Genuine interest, satisfaction, ability to discuss sexual issues . . . these are characteristics of a sexually intimate relationship.

4. Intellectual intimacy. Intellectual intimacy involves the sharing of ideas. In short, when you are intellectually intimate you talk to each other. More than just superficial conversations about the weather, you seek input from your mate regarding issues of importance. You value your mate's opinion and want to share your own. There is an attitude of mutual respect. Feeling "put down," feeling conversations are futile, feeling as though your mate is constantly trying to change your ideas . . . these are absent in intellectually intimate relationships. Instead, conversations are stimulating and enriching.

5. *Recreational intimacy.* When you are recreationally intimate, you enjoy and share in many of the same "just for fun" activities. You have many similar interests. Whether it be outdoor activities or indoor, you like "playing" together. Even in the midst of hectic schedules, you find time to do fun things. And in so doing, you feel closer to one another.

6. *Spiritual intimacy.* For you to be spiritually intimate, three criteria must be met:

   a. you must share common or similar beliefs about God;
   b. these beliefs must be important or significant to your lives; and
   c. you must honestly share where each one of you is in your own spiritual quest.

Having only one or two of these prerequisites to spiritual intimacy will not do. All must be present. Those of you who have been raised in the same denomination and who personally value your religious commitment may be no more intimate spiritually than others who are unequally yoked if you do not share your journey with one another. Dutiful attendance at religious activities is no guarantee that spiritual intimacy exists within a marriage. This form of closeness requires much more.

Recognizing true marital intimacy for what it really is—having many dimensions—is a real breakthrough. It gives us a greater understanding of what it takes to make a marriage work. No longer do we view closeness as a singular attainment. Rather, true closeness is now seen as the presence of multiple intimacies . . . not just one. In fact, the greater the number of dimensions in which we find ourselves to be intimate, the greater the degree of total intimacy within our marriage.

Some of you may want your marriage to succeed, yet you desire to be intimate in only one dimension of the relationship. For example, you may desire sexual intimacy but care little about intellectual, social, emotional, recreational, or spiritual aspects of the relationship. This approach to marriage is destined to failure. Your marriage may not end in divorce but it will fail just the same. You cannot expect to be truly close if you are trying to be only sexually intimate.

I recently counseled a couple who had this very problem. Actually, the husband's desire was more singularly focused than his wife's. But his interest in only one dimension, at the exclusion of the others, presented the relationship with a great deal of difficulty. Lisa summed it up very well:

> Tim and I are emotional strangers. We have no idea who we are anymore. When he's not at the office, he's either working in the yard or on the golf course. We never spend any time together.
>
> Tim isn't cruel to me. In fact, in a lot of ways he is an ideal husband. He's responsible, dependable . . . what more could you want?
>
> Well . . . I'll tell you what I want. I want someone who will talk to me; someone who will listen; someone who wants to be with me somewhere besides in bed. For six years it seems as though all I have been good for is sex. Well, now I'm not even good for that. I'm tired and fed up. I'm just not interested in it anymore.

For six years Tim had been a responsible husband. To use Lisa's words, he was nearly "ideal." But he had not been intimate. In fact, the only way in which he desired to be "close" to Lisa was sexually. The result was a drifting marriage.

If husbands are going to choose only one area to be intimate with their wives, it is usually this one. Some men simply do not know how to relate intimately to a woman in any other manner. It seems to be easier to go to bed with someone than it is to talk about your fears or to share your dreams. For example, it was difficult for Tim to draw close to Lisa, so he preoccupied himself with other admirable activities. Fortunately for the marriage, both Lisa and Tim were willing to work at changing the flow of their relationship. They both agreed to a short-term contract which structured how they related to one another. As a part of the agreement, the number of occasions in which they could be sexually active during the week was limited. The contract required that they spend at least thirty minutes in significant conversation before they could be sexually intimate and the conversation had to take place in a room other than the bedroom. They were given exercises to aid in this time of emotional and intellectual sharing.

Some interesting changes began to occur as Lisa and Tim implemented this new structure. As Tim began to share himself emotionally and intellectually with Lisa, his need for sex decreased. It didn't disappear by any means, but it did recede to a level more normal than what it had been. Also, he began to feel more comfortable in his sharing.

For Lisa, there was also a change in her interest in sex. Rather than decreasing as it had for Tim, she found that her desire actually increased. Her interest had returned.

Emotional closeness, intellectual closeness, spiritual closeness . . . absence of these relegates sex to only a physical act. And as only a physical act, its enjoyment and/or contribution to the relationship is lessened. This is what had happened to Lisa and Tim. With the multidimensional quality of intimacy, failure to grow together is actually the result of multiple failures. By failing to be intimate in any of these essential dimensions, contribution is made toward failure in the whole.

The Importance of Planning

Why is this nonintimate situation so prevalent? Why is it that couples are so willing to settle for this lesser form of marriage? Why are countless scores of couples drifting instead of achieving the intimacy so desired and expected?

It is not that people marry lacking good intentions. Think back to when you were "nearly weds." Remember the excitement? Remember the anticipated fulfillment to come from your being joined together? I do. Moonstruck, starry-eyed, smitten . . . these are the terms which describe the manner in which we viewed life and our future together. It's no different today. We still enter marriage with great expectations. Typically we marry genuinely desiring to be good husbands and wives. Each husband truly intends to give. Each wife desires to meet her husband's needs. Yet, even with hopeful optimism and ecstatic anticipation, the majority of these marriages fail. Though well-intended, their initial drive dissipates. Failure will be their destination. Why? Part of the reason is this:

All couples marry *intending* to be happy. . . .
Few marry *planning* to be happy.

The key to achieving intimacy in marriage is PLANNING. My use of planning is not in its more restrictive sense. Rigid planning can be viewed as clear-cut schedules; orderly arrangements of parts and pieces; precise executions of specified events and activities. The more flexible quality of planning is what appeals to me. Not the harsh rigidity of scheduling but the softer emphasis of method. To plan is "to have a method for carrying out a design or for doing something."

My personal goal is to have an intimate relationship with my wife. I do not want to drift. To reach my goal, I have to plan. I have to have a method. As a counselor, I realize far too well the consequences of failing to plan. I know the ease in which interferences crop up to prevent me from getting what I want. It is this realization that forces me to methodically attend to my marriage. I plan to work at it . . . to invest in it . . . to make an effort.

I do not deal with problems as they arise because it is easy or because it is comfortable. Most of the time it would be easier to avoid some of these conflicts and problems but I recognize the consequences of avoidance—the distancing, the coldness, the indifference. I do not want these saboteurs to creep into my marriage, progressively destroying that which I hold most dear. With the emotional distance would come a movement toward a drifting, failing scenario, but because of the importance placed on my marital relationship, I methodically deal with issues as they arise. I am not willing to settle for a lesser form of marriage.

It would be easy for me to become wrapped up or overinvolved in my work. I have spent many years preparing for my profession. By constantly following the theme of greatest interest, I have selectively narrowed my career field. The result is that I have successfully created, for me at least, work which is not work. Marriage counseling is a love.

Being a love, counseling has the potential for creating difficulty in my marriage. It could become a mistress. It would be very easy for me to work at the office all day and come home in the evening only to continue my work. I love to write, to read, to create, to research, to. . . . Remember, for me, this is *not* work. Even if not actually working in my study, I have been known to be present in bodily form only to have my mind many miles away. I think Jan finds this even more offensive than my actual bodily absence from the home.

As you can see, the type of interest and dedication which may be good for my career can paradoxically wreak havoc with my marriage. To counter this tendency requires planning. I have to work at placing my marriage in a priority position. I have to consciously contend with these pitfalls. I have had to develop my own personal method, something particularly suited to me, in order to move toward my goal . . . an intimate relationship. You will have to do the same.

True success is never an easy achievement. Happy and fulfilling marriages are products of extreme effort. They are desired, sought after, fought for, and planned. They never *just* happen. Couples frequently complain to me how their marriage *just* fell apart. All of a sudden, they just fell out of love . . . just lost interest in a husband . . . just fell in love with another person or career. If experience has taught me anything, it is this: Nothing *just* happens . . . whether good or bad.

Healthy marriages follow a road . . . a road that is planned. You do not have to plan to fail. That can be accomplished without planning . . . and usually is. But you DO have to plan to succeed.

I think that at least part of our difficulty rests with the nearsighted vision of near-to-weds. They seemingly cannot see beyond the immediate goal of *getting married* to the truer goal of *building a relationship*. In reality, the marital ceremony is the beginning . . . not a climax. It is the beginning of a process . . . a process that will lead to either an intimate and vibrant relationship or a dry and barren shell.

Intimate experiences occur spontaneously, such as an unintended sharing of harbored emotions, prompting compassion from your mate . . . an accidental time together without the children, allowing tender reflections on past hopes and dreams . . . a refreshing romantic interlude occurring when the routine has been unavoidably interrupted. We have all experienced these unexpected boons. These and other unplanned, uncalculated, and unpredicted occurrences can sprinkle our lives with momentary pleasure. They are brief glimpses, as it were, of a far better existence, but they are not the sum and substance of an intimate relationship.

Intimate relationships are built. They are the by-product of conscious effort. They do not occur spontaneously, rather, they develop with the aid of time. Consistent investment in the marriage, spread over years of time, will pay high dividends. Couples who are working at building an intimate relationship actively:

- *Accept responsibility* for their portion of the relationship, choosing to deal with problems as opposed to comfortably avoiding them.
- *Prioritize* their life-style, giving each other time and ensuring that the relationship does not get "second best."
- *Relate* in an emotionally honest manner as opposed to superficially.
- *Evaluate* their relationship, determining where it is going and what they can do to control the direction.
- *Recognize*, acknowledge, and attend to each other's needs.

These aspects, thoughtfully planned and executed, are some of the prerequisites for building a healthy marriage.

Diagnosis Is the Easy Part

As a marriage counselor, I find the diagnostic aspect of my work to be the simplest. The diagnostic portion is where I determine what the problem with the marriage is and what has caused it. Diagnostic ease has not always been the case for me. In fact, when I first began my work as a counselor, I found diagnosis to be a very difficult task. Marriage seemed to be so complex (it was and still is). There were always so many variables involved . . . so many factors to be considered. I found it difficult to sort through all of the possible interferences. I would literally end some sessions in bewilderment, asking myself the question, "What in the world is going on here?"

Over the years, things gradually changed. After working with many couples, and with the addition of some fairly intensive training, I arrived at a point where diagnosis really became the simpler of my duties. As it stands now, after about an hour of working with a couple, I generally have a pretty good idea of what has been going on in the marriage and what they need to do in order to change their relationship. It is then that I encounter the truly difficult part of counseling . . . getting them to do it.

The art of counseling is not in diagnosis. Granted, this is an essential first step. There must be a clear and concise definition of both the problem and its cause. Yet, the true art of counseling is in getting couples to do what they need to do. Changing behavior is the real task and it is not easy.

Developing an intimate marital relationship presents us with much the same kind of paradox. It is simple, but it is not easy. We know what it takes to build a healthy marriage. That's simple. You give, you share, you prioritize, etc. There is no great mystical secret to be discovered. We understand all of this. We just keep failing to do it.

In the following section, I have attempted to thoroughly describe each of the primary contributors to drifting. As we become more aware of them, we can be more on guard. I have also provided exercises to aid in the personal self-assessment of your own marriage. In some instances, I have even given tasks to aid you in changing some of the more nonproductive aspects of your relationship. I have done all this realizing that it is far simpler for me to tell you what needs to be done than it will be for you to do it.

Change will not be easy. But few things worth having are ever easily achieved. Having a healthy marriage is no exception. Marriage is the most significant earthly relationship we will ever encounter. It is undoubtedly the most demanding, designed to be the most rewarding, yet having the potential for being the most frustrating. Which of these goals you achieve will be greatly determined by whether or not your marriage drifts. And whether or not your marriage drifts will be greatly determined by how you deal with each of the following contributors. The responsibility is yours . . . as are the rewards.

PART TWO
CONTRIBUTORS TO DRIFTING

— 4 —
AVOIDING SENSITIVE ISSUES

Most people in our society marry for intimacy. Maybe not everyone, but the vast majority of us wed with the anticipation that we will obtain emotional closeness. This expectation is normal, healthy, and definitely a part of the Lord's design for man's companionship. An excessively high divorce rate merely confirms the fact that many of us are failing to achieve the degree of intimacy we so longingly desire. The satisfactions, the rewards, and the gains have all been painfully elusive.

Growing together in a manner which forms a healthy and enriching marriage is a challenge. Many factors can obstinately emerge within a relationship to thwart the development of intimacy.

Although it would be possible to develop a long and extensive list of contributors, there are some whose frequency and persistence qualify them to be referred to as "common." One of these common inhibitors to emotional closeness, and therefore a contributor to drifting, is the tendency for mates to avoid sensitive issues.

The avoidance of sensitive issues actually has two components:

1. The fact that mates do have sensitive issues.
2. The fact that these issues are sometimes avoided.

In regard to the first component, having sensitive issues is quite normal. All couples have them. Whether it is your marriage, my marriage, or anyone else's marriage, there are issues within them which create a great deal of discomfort.

These sensitivities create stress—both within us personally and within our relationship—and we do not like stress. We bristle. We become tense. We become nervous and anxious. Emotional anguish and pain seem to permeate the air.

For some of us it is sex, for others in-laws. "Why can't we ever talk about the kids without fighting?" "Even though we go to church every week, why do we avoid discussion of all but the most superficial spiritual matters?" A truly comprehensive list would be exhaustive. Furthermore, the old adage "What is one man's drink is another man's poison" is also very appropriate here. What presents no problem at all for some of us may prove devastating for others. But regardless of the fact that these issues will vary from couple to couple, it must be reaffirmed that we are all still endowed with them. What seems to be most important here is not that these issues exist, but rather, how they are handled. This brings us to the second component of our problem.

Not only do all couples have these touchy subjects, but all couples avoid them from time to time. No matter how healthy or unhealthy the relationship . . . whether it is your marriage, my marriage, or anyone else's marriage, there are things not talked about . . . issues not dealt with . . . and topics that are shunned. The discomfort and pain prompt us to avoid them. It seems only reasonable. No one enjoys pain. No one likes to be hurt. When confronted with discomfort, our natural tendency is to be "pain free." So, just as it is normal for sensitive issues to be present in our marriages, it is also normal for us to try to avoid them.

I need at this time to distinguish between "behaviors" and "patterns," for it is with this difference that the problem of avoidance truly rests. Behaviors are individual and separate actions. They can be fairly spontaneous and nonpredictable. A counselor learns early in his career not to place much stock in a one-time observance of a particular behavior. A man who shouts at his wife is not necessarily an insensitive tyrant. If an individual or couple is watched for a long period of time, almost any behavior is likely to be observed. What does begin to capture our attention, however, are those behaviors which are observed repeatedly.

Frequency is the distinguishing characteristic between an action being merely a behavior or a significant pattern. It is patterns which concern us. Within marriages, what proves to be unhealthy and counterproductive are not the isolated incidences of avoidance. We expect to see these occasionally. Rather, what truly plagues couples are patterns . . . the repetitive use of avoidance behaviors. These patterns are predictable. Healthy relationships are not exempt from avoidance behavior . . . they just utilize it less often.

Avoidance Strategies

In my marriage counseling career, I have observed five patterns or strategies commonly used by couples to avoid sensitive issues. To emphasize a point, I am using the terms *patterns* and *strategies* interchangeably, even though their true definitions are somewhat different. The term *pattern* evokes little emotional connotation from us. It is fairly objective. It denotes description. We get the feeling that something merely exists. *Strategy*, on the other hand, captures our emotions. It implies some degree of deviousness . . . some effort at cooperative planning . . . a sinister plot. It is this aspect of cooperation which I want to emphasize.

Within relationships, all patterns are strategies. They are all products of cooperative effort. Although sometimes unaware of their actions, **each mate** works to maintain the particular patterns which exist in their marriage. This point will become clearer a little later when we look at some of the specific avoidance strategies. But for the time being, I want you to be cognizant of the fact that, without the repetitive, cooperative, and predictable efforts of **both mates**, the patterns would not exist. This is true for you as well. For a consistent pattern of interaction to exist within your marriage, it must be maintained by the efforts of *both* you and your mate.

Deeply ingrained patterns of avoidance are nothing more than relational games. Like all other games, these too have rules. These rules govern how you behave toward one another when you play your avoidance game. If you abide by the rules, you are able to maintain the game. Maintaining the game allows you to reach your goal. And of course, your goal is to avoid the sensitive issue.

Each of you has a role. Each has a part. If one of you were to change your role, the game could no longer be played. New rules would have to be developed. This is why I refer to these as strategies.

Strategy #1 "We just don't talk about it." Probably the most obvious avoidance strategy is simply to never bring the issue up for discussion. Never means *never*. You just never talk about sex in your home; or question where the marriage is going; or express your concern about needs that are not getting met; or how in-laws are interfering in divisive ways; or, for that matter, anything else of significance. "We just don't talk about it." You do not bring it up and your mate does not bring it up. You cooperate. You work together to avoid a tense encounter. You usually know you are avoiding but you do it anyway. Sometimes you even feel very justified in avoiding issues in this manner.

- "Think of the hostility that would be created if we discussed it."
- "I'm really helping to preserve my marriage by not bringing it up."
- "It wouldn't get settled anyway."

One counselor has said, "If you can think of a subject that you and your spouse have not talked about recently, it is probably the very thing you need to deal with the most." Just because something isn't discussed by people does not mean that it is not standing between them.

An issue that is avoided in this manner may not come up in your conversations but it is ever present in your thoughts. You dwell on it . . . mull it over . . . are sometimes nearly possessed by it. The hurt eats away like a cancer. You are miserable. Not discussed, yet definitely present. Never confronted and never resolved. So goes the strategy of not talking about it. Can you see how this pattern contributes to the tendency to drift?

Strategy #2 Withdrawal of one spouse.   This second strategy is closely related to the first. The major difference is that, instead of having two mates who are unwilling to bring up a topic, we now have only one. While one pretends the problem does not exist, the other refuses to deny its presence. The result is similar to a game of tennis where you have one player who serves the ball and the other who refuses to return the volley.

If you are creative, you can cooperatively develop any number of variations of this strategy. One way to play this game is to pretend to be disinterested in what is being said. "Did you say something, dear?" If used consistently, your mate can quickly learn that this is his or her cue to drop the subject. Your pseudodisinterest clearly conveys this message. Although not as offending as some of the other variations, the goal is the same . . . avoidance.

A more offensive variation of this strategy is for you to be totally nonresponsive. Whatever your mate says is greeted with complete and absolute silence. The emotional intent of your nonresponse will follow one of two general themes. You may perceive yourself locked into some kind of power struggle. Your response then reflects an "I'll show you" attitude. You have learned that by silently going about your business, you get not only the last word but generally an emotionally frustrated reaction as well. Neither screaming and hollering nor crying and begging make any real difference. You cannot be swayed.

Nonchalantly, you discount and ignore your mate's total presence. Without saying a word, you loudly proclaim, "You do not count." Even if not on the outside, there is at least a smile on the inside. You are definitely winning this round.

The other general theme found in a response of absolute silence is far less vindictive than that of the power struggle described above. It is best capsulized by the statement, "Gee, I just don't know what to say." The sequence goes something like this: In silence, you listen to your mate with much intensity. You appear to be evaluating every word that is being said. You project concern and caring. Your expression changes as your mate continues. But finally the talking stops and you do not respond. There is a long pause. The silence becomes deafening.

You have listened. You are concerned. You would even like to respond. But you do not know what to say. You are still thinking about it. You are still evaluating. You are taking what was said to heart. You need only to assess it for a while . . . at least a day or two. Time passes as your emotional system experiences an override. It is as if you have totally shut down.

Finally, the vacuum of silence is broken—not with a response to what has been said, but with some form of diversion. You look away; you pick up the newspaper; you begin watching television; you leave the room; you begin talking about something else, etc. There are many diversions that will work. The end result, however, is always the same. Silence has won out. Normal activity is resumed. Whatever it was that had paramount importance has been avoided. If it is to be dealt with, it will have to be at another time and place . . . a time and place which will probably continue to elude you.

Another variation of this strategy is for you to physically withdraw. This can be negotiated with varying degrees of tact and dramatization. For instance, you may casually move from one room to another. This can be most smoothly executed when there is a legitimate diversion in the other room such as a television program, the children, or tasks which are demanding attention. It may be a convenient time to run to the store or even take a walk. If you wish to have the last word without saying it and still let it be known that you do not wish to discuss the topic, you need only to slam a door on your way out. This form of behavior often rings of the power struggle discussed above.

Truly the most sophisticated use of this strategy would find you saying something like, "Yes, dear, I have a similar concern. Why don't we talk about it later?" Isn't that smooth? Of course, no appointment is set and "later" never comes. The issue is not resolved . . . just forgotten.

Although my emphasis with this strategy has been in the description of the withdrawing mate, we must not forget that both mates have a role in maintaining this particular avoidance pattern. Perhaps the issue is brought up in a manner which is guaranteed to prompt the withdrawal of a well-conditioned mate. Vehement attacks, well-calculated barbs, degrading observations . . . no one responds well to these. Perhaps the disparaged partner's withdrawal is anticipated. Perhaps it is even the goal. But even though this more devious variation does occur, it is more the exception than the rule.

Most of the initiating mates honestly want to deal with the problem and most of the withdrawing mates do not. That being the case, what are the rules by which this game is played? In an abbreviated format, the rules which regulate the game are these:

Mate A: initiates discussion regarding a sensitive issue.

Mate B: responds by withdrawing in one manner or another.

Mate A: responds by willingly allowing the issue to be dropped.

Those are the rules. Each of you has a role. Each of you has had a part. With the issue willingly dropped, it is soon "business as usual." Soon, the superficial cordiality which permeates the relationship is resumed. We need only to watch for a while to see the entire drama reenacted.

Strategy #3 Changing the topic. Of all the strategies, this is the one I have personally mastered the best. Or, should I say, it has mastered me. Like an old athletic injury, it spontaneously reappears in times of interpersonal stress. Predictably, it is there.

In trying to uncover its lineage, I find that I actually acquired this tendency many years ago in my own home and family. (That's where you learned yours as well.) My learning was not necessarily through well-modeled parental behaviors. Nor was it by their conscious design. Just the same, through the everyday experiences which came from being a part of a family emotional system, I learned that changing the subject was an effective means of avoiding some of the pressure which came my way.

As bad a habit as it may be, it has followed me into adulthood. Persistently and unconsciously, it tries to remain a part of my present relationships. Training and experience have convinced me that there is no undesirable tendency so strong that it cannot be improved with appropriate corrective actions. With intentional corrective persistence, this personal strategy is gradually diminishing in influence upon my relationships.

Appropriately and skillfully used, this strategy can quickly get you "off the spot." You know how it works. You and your mate are intently discussing a significant issue in your marriage. Your mate then says something that is direct and too much to the point. Your response (casually, coolly, and calmly) is: "What do you want to do with the kids this Saturday?" The kids weren't the issue. Saturday wasn't the issue. Being together as a family wasn't the issue. But if you can make the creative leap from what was being discussed to this new subject, the sensitive issue will have been avoided. The intensity of the conversation will change. Your cold sweat will disappear. Your respiration will return to a normal rate and, to some degree, the anxious and uncomfortable feelings which were beginning to overwhelm you will subside.

To dissect the sequence as we have done here gives this strategy the appearance of disjointed and abrupt interchanges between two individuals. You are probably thinking, *Surely, intelligent people would not be susceptible to this pattern.* Wrong. First of all, intelligence has very little to do with the development and maintenance of avoidance strategies. Whether it be this or any other pattern, we are all participants in emotional games. Second, in real life, strategies are executed with effortless ease and smoothness. The disjointed abruptness brought about by our examination is only an illusion. Practice upon practice has resulted in execution with precision. Like the graceful ease of a well-trained relay team, the baton is flawlessly passed. Coolly, calmly, precisely . . . without a second thought, the baton is passed and, at least relationally, the goal has been achieved. Safely, we have arrived at a less sensitive topic.

Being imaginative creatures, we will often interject slight variations to this game so as to be able to call it uniquely ours. Some of you may use strategic pauses. Others may employ humor or laughter as a transitional mechanism from one subject to another. Whatever the modifications imposed by a particular style, the effectiveness of changing the subject cannot be denied. Without premeditation, without hesitancy, and without difficulty, an issue which needs attention is abandoned for one which does not. So goes the strategy.

As with all strategies, each of you has a role. Each of you has a part to be played. With this particular strategy, the two roles are obvious: one of you changes the subject and the other allows it to be changed. It is as simple as that. If the subject changer were to modify his role, the game would not be played. If the allowing partner were to change his role, the game would stop. But neither of you do, so the game proceeds. So goes the world of strategies.

Strategy #4 Agreeing too easily.   To many, this seems to be an unlikely strategy. The mere suggestion that agreement may be a culprit, as opposed to an aid, is generally met with surprise. Perhaps this is why it is so effective as an avoidance tactic.

Do we not strive for agreement between mates? Is not cooperation our goal? Do we not labor and wrestle with sensitive issues in the hopes that some form of resolution will be attained? To all of these I would have to agree. Although we would be somewhat remiss to perceive these as our only relational goals, there is no denying that these are admirable and to be sought after. If this is the case, then where is the problem?

Problems come with the ease in which agreement is given. How honest is the supposed resolve? Did the acquiescing mate truly mean what he said or did he have an ulterior motive? Is there an unstated goal to which he is aspiring? These are cynical questions. Yet, they speak to the heart of this strategy. Agreement which is reached too easily is not truly agreement—it is a sham.

As with other strategies, this one has a couple of variations. One is illustrated by this conversation between an irritated wife and her "on the spot" husband.

Wife: "I've told you time and time again that I don't want you taking my mother's side when she and I are having a disagreement."

Husband: "You're absolutely right. I'll never do it again."

With this brief interchange, the issue is dropped. As you are beginning to realize, being "dropped" and being "settled" are not the same thing. In this case, the interfering mate isn't really going to change anything that's being done. The next time his wife and mother-in-law have a disagreement, he'll be found in the middle of it. But, at least for the present moment, he has avoided having to deal with his wife over his interfering behavior. True to form, this tactic of agreeing too easily has gotten him conveniently off the hot spot. He will never interfere again—until next time. So goes the game.

There is a second variation of this strategy. Your mate becomes extremely upset with you, blows up, and storms off. Some time later, he returns very apologetically. With a mellowed disposition, he tenderly states, "I'm sorry, dear. I just got angry."

He does have a way with words, doesn't he? That short statement is intended to be a cure-all. No further discussion is supposed to take place. Everything is now okay. Do not return to the precipitating issue. Do not discuss how this blowup affected your feelings. Do not do anything except get things back to normal. And that is exactly what happens . . . business as usual.

Needless to say, this variation of agreeing or giving in too easily can have many unwanted repercussions. But that won't change the pattern. The game will continue to be reenacted.

As has been my custom, I wish to emphasize that each of you has had a part in maintaining this strategy. Each plays a role. In your own way, each is responsible. One disgruntled wife recently complained to me about her husband of 35 years. Vividly she described how, throughout the entirety of their married life, he had managed to elude all but the most insignificant responsibilities. She would ask him to see that something was done. His immediate and standard response was always, "I'll take care of it." I asked her what would happen then. She responded, "What do you think? Bills wouldn't get paid. Leaks would get bigger. Grass would grow higher." I then asked what would happen next. Her response was very revealing: "Why, I paid the bills, called the plumber, and mowed the grass."

I'll let you figure out what was going on here. As I have said, it takes two to maintain any pattern. Each partner has a role. Each mate has a part. Have you begun to look at yours yet?

Strategy #5 Arguing. Marital partners who argue do so for many different reasons. In some marriages it is a way of life. Yelling, shouting, hurling demeaning statements—these are the standard tools for dealing with any problem. Nothing is ever discussed or evaluated on its own merits. Seldom is there peaceful disagreement.

The awareness of this life-style is commonly admitted by those who possess it. Sometimes it is confessed in a sobering tone: "We never seem to get anywhere. We just argue." "When we fight, we say things we don't mean. We usually end up hurting each other." Other couples project an almost boastful air: "We fight like cats and dogs. I guess neither of us would really have it any other way."

This particular life-style or form of interaction is obvious but Christian couples are seldom plagued by the obvious. In Christian homes, it is not the "way of life" argumentative style which presents difficulty. The Christian variation is far more sporadic and lacks the constancy of the secular counterpart. Its occurrence has a far more occasional quality compared to the generalized across-the-board characteristic exhibited by the "way of life" couples.

This comparison is not meant to bring you comfort or to make you feel good because you only argue occasionally. "Occasional" is not the goal. Granted, it is the rare couple who would go throughout their entire married life without at least an occasional quarrel. But our concern is with patterns and not isolated behaviors. Is arguing being employed in a devious manner? Is there a pattern?

What are the rules to the game? Is the occasional use of arguing precipitated by a reoccurring issue or situation? Where does communication break down? When and why do you move from negotiating to arguing?

At least part of the answer lies with avoidance. As with the previous four strategies, arguing can be an effective means of avoiding sensitive issues. It is truly amazing how we can argue and argue and never deal with the real issue. What generally happens when we argue is that we get *off* the topic and *on to* each other. We begin to tear each other down. This brings out some powerful emotions. The result: we have effectively avoided a sensitive issue.

What I am suggesting when I refer to arguing as a strategy is that, for some of us, it is a goal and not a by-product. As a goal it allows us to satisfactorily avoid something of a sensitive nature and we have found that it is far better to argue than to deal directly with the topic.

It's amazing to think that for some of us, arguing is less painful than discussion. But for some of us, that's the way it is. To give up this style of interaction would mean to come face-to-face with this pain. Therefore, we cooperatively maintain this game. Knowing that we should not argue does not seem to help much. All we know is that we cannot seem to help ourselves. Caught in the rules, the roles will continue to be reenacted.

All of the strategies mentioned above are interaction styles or relational games. We use them to successfully avoid dealing with sensitive matters. Some of these patterns are so deeply ingrained and such a part of the way in which we relate to each other that the roles are acted out with little or no forethought. Automatically, the subject is changed, an argument begins, we withdraw, etc. Unintentionally, the game begins. But regardless of the intent, the consequences of these patterns are the same—emotional distance in the relationship which encourages us to drift.

Misconceptions

For the sake of clarification, there are two issues which need to be addressed. First of all, to enter a relationship under the assumption that every difficulty between you and your mate will be resolved is an error. Not everything will be resolved just because you deal with it . . . at least, not initially. Some issues may require repeated attempts. There are issues with which my wife and I have dealt repeatedly throughout the years of our marriage. They are almost old friends. They are not yet resolved, but they are better. We just keep chipping away at them.

Second, do not confuse my emphasis on interactional patterns and relational games with the many variations of communication skills training commonly available today. There is a vast degree of difference between these two areas. To focus on the rules which govern how mates interact with one another is to deal with what is *wrong* with their present communication. These relational rules prevent good communication from occurring. Couples are bound by them and become virtual prisoners of them. Held captive by things seemingly beyond their control, they are powerless to change.

Communication skills training, on the other hand, focuses on what mates ought to be saying to one another. It describes the *right* way to communicate. If marital partners would only follow the well-intended instructions of those who teach communication skills, communication would be far more productive. As asserted by the instructors, "All they have to do is implement the change."

Although some individuals may benefit from such training, many will have a difficult time simply replacing what is wrong with what is right. What is wrong—the deeply engrained avoidance patterns, rules, games—is tenacious. It will not be easily replaced. I believe it is far more productive when what is wrong is corrected *before* what is right is implemented. If the faulty interactional patterns can be identified and interrupted, their replacement with more constructive alternatives will be a more achievable task.

What You Can Do

Any couple who desires to improve their marriage can do so. The following suggestions will help reduce nonproductive avoidance strategies which interfere with the development of true intimacy.

Assess Your Situation

What are the sensitive issues in your relationship? How do you and your mate work together to avoid dealing with them? Who does what? What are the rules which control your game? Remember, it takes two to maintain any interactional pattern.

Working independently, you and your mate can make two lists. The first list will be of the sensitive issues that you perceive to exist in your relationship. Your second list will consist of the strategies you and your mate use to avoid dealing with these issues. After completing the lists, exchange them and discuss your findings.

A funny thing occurs when we begin to identify and discuss our strategies. *Once we learn the rules, it is harder to play the game.* The unintentional and habitual now become recognized. The covert becomes overt. Once we see what it is that we are doing, it is harder to abide by the old rules. To continue in the old game would require that we become intentional and knowledgeable participants. Therefore, recognition is the beginning of change.

Commit Yourself to Change

Recognition may be the first step, but a *commitment to change* is an essential second step. This is best accomplished by developing a plan of action. I like the saying, "If things aren't going according to plan, it might be that there never was a plan."

As I have already stated, all couples marry *intending* to be happy. Few *plan* for it. To change the way in which we relate to one another requires intentional effort—a plan of action.

Although change is difficult, it is not impossible. A good rule of thumb in developing your plan of action is to "do something different." If you tend to withdraw, try not to leave the scene. If you tend to get into heated arguments, make a date to return later. When cooler heads prevail, affirm your love for each other and then deal with the real issue. If one person is a better talker, you may wish to sit back-to-back for twenty minutes, allowing each an uninterrupted 10-minute opportunity to express a position. Be creative. Your options are limitless.

Do not expect things to change instantaneously. It has taken many years to develop your unique style. It will take some time to correct it. It is best if you and your mate can agree on what to do. However, if this is not the case, remember that biblically we are only responsible for our own behavior. I have seen many instances where change in one partner brought change in a mate. For the game to be maintained, *both* must continue to play by the rules. A sustained change in one mate will prevent the game from continuing in its present form. This can then result in a positive impact on the marriage.

As you are forced to deal with problems and conflicts, an amazing thing will occur. You will find yourselves becoming closer. There will be more intimacy . . . more growth . . . more genuine concern. And with this, your relationship will move from one drifting into destruction to one with greater intimacy and personal satisfaction.

— 5 —
SENSITIVITY
AND
INSENSITIVITY

Another common inhibitor to emotional closeness, and therefore a contributor to drifting, is insensitivity. In fact, from my perspective, there is probably no other element more devastating to a marital relationship than this one. Nothing more effectively eats away at the "ties that bind" than the perception that what you say doesn't seem to matter. Commitments, vows, spoken pledges . . . all the things upon which a love was based . . . gradually fade as personal needs, desires, and feelings are consistently denied or discounted by a once-admired mate.

The quality of a marriage can be measured by the sensitivity displayed between the mates. Those in troubled marriages quickly point to insensitivity as the rule and not an exception. When couples come to me for counseling, they frequently feel uncared for. During the counseling sessions, anger and hurt permeate the atmosphere. Eagerly, one insensitive instance after another is described.

When both partners believe they have been victimized, the session resembles a boxing match. With reckless abandon, each mate viciously scores points with verbal punches and jabs. When only one mate feels uncared for, counseling has a different flow. Unlike the boxers mentioned above, a pattern having one mate as an attacker and the other as a denier emerges. Often, the denier "discounts" until the bitter end.

Both sets of couples go to great lengths to describe the alleged insensitivities. Some of the recounted deeds are blatant. "He said he was going to do it regardless of what I wanted to do. He said that if I didn't like it, I could leave!" Others are not so obvious. They are the passive neglects. They are the needs of which, although recognized, nothing is said or done. To not respond *is* a response and a passive response of this nature is one of insensitivity.

Some acts of insensitivity are intentional, deliberate misdeeds. Others are accidental. Some are admitted while still others are denied. But regardless of intent or design, one thing is certain— insensitivity does a great deal toward destroying a marriage.

Since as a counselor I have been invited into relationships as an intimate observer, up to this point I have been describing some of the situations I have seen in my practice. It would be an error, however, to think that insensitivity exists only in couples who seek marital counseling. For *most* marriages insensitivity, regardless of the manner in which it is expressed, remains a genuine threat.

What is there about insensitivity that makes it so lethal? Why is it so powerful . . . so destructive? Upon what is its effectiveness based? I believe that at the heart of insensitivity there is a statement which rocks the foundation of the marriage and proclaims, "I don't care about you!"

Nothing damages a relationship more dramatically than this perception. Regardless of the manner in which this is conveyed, believing that you are not cared for by your mate destroys the foundation of the relationship.

Those who sense that they are uncared for experience a number of feelings and repercussions.

1. They feel *rejected*. Being rejected creates feelings of hurt and anger. As these mount, the angry mate becomes resentful. This general tone of hostility often emerges as "resistance" within the relationship.

2. They feel *helpless*. When a mate "doesn't care," there is a sense of being out of control. Uncared-for partners often feel powerless to change things. They are confused, frustrated, and anxious. They cannot demand caring. What is there left to do? Nothing.

3. They feel *hopeless*. Since their mate does not truly care for them, they see very little hope for the relationship. Truly, what can they do? Any efforts would be only futile attempts. Without hope, motivation is destroyed. They soon have no "willingness" to work toward a more satisfying relationship. They resign themselves to drift.

Is there any wonder why insensitivity can be such an effective threat to the success of marriage?

Insensitivity is a threat, but it would be a mistake to describe it as an undefeatable foe. It is powerful, but conquerable. To defeat insensitivity we must have a better understanding of what it is and how it unobservably takes control of a relationship. That is the goal of this chapter. Through (1) definition, (2) recognition of its many variations or forms, (3) realization of consequences, and (4) identification of constructive challenges, the effectiveness of insensitivity is reduced.

Insensitivity Defined

Insensitivity means different things to different people. Even within the context of a marital relationship, there can be great diversity in its definition. It is most easily understood by first considering the meaning of its root word, *sensitivity*.

Broadly stated, *sensitivity* refers to the capacity of an organism to both receive and respond to stimulation. As we narrow our use of sensitivity to the specific confines of the marital relationship, we find the following definition to be appropriate.

Marital *sensitivity*: The recognition of and response
to the needs and desires of a mate.

At this point it is crucial that the twofold nature of sensitivity be recognized. If you will take a moment to reread the definition, you will notice that sensitivity actually has two parts or elements. A mate *recognizes* and a mate *responds*.

To be sensitive, the needs and desires of a mate must first be recognized. A sensitive mate must first hear what is being said. To hear requires one to listen . . . often with the heart as well as the ears. The true concern of the message must be sensed. Feelings have to be perceived and desires recognized. Sometimes the needs are of an ego nature, for example, of affirmation, acknowledgment, emotional support, and valuing. Sometimes the needs take a more tangible bent such as cooperating together to achieve tasks and goals like sharing child-care responsibilities. At times, these needs (whether ego or tangible) are conveyed with the use of words. At other times, not a word is spoken. What is important, however, is that they be recognized. Without recognition, there can be no sensitivity.

Once recognized, the perceived needs and desires must be met with a response. Respond is an action word. To respond means that something is done. The particular something is largely dependent upon the specific need or desire expressed by the mate. It may be something physical like a touch, a hug, or a kiss. It may be acknowledgment of an idea, a fear, or a joy. Smiles can be sensitive responses as can merely taking time to be a sounding board. Some needs and desires may require a more active response. Need for the redistribution of household responsibilities requires negotiation and a great deal of effort. But regardless of the need or desire, being sensitive always necessitates a response.

Erroneously, sensitivity is sometimes thought of as being one or the other . . . either recognition *or* response. A truly sensitive mate does not *either* recognize or respond to the needs of his marital partner. He does BOTH.

With marital sensitivity defined, let's proceed to the definition of marital insensitivity.

Marital *insensitivity:* The failure to either recognize or respond to the needs and desires of a mate.

Isn't it interesting? To be sensitive requires that you both recognize *and* respond. Yet, to be insensitive requires only that you fail to do one *or* the other. Failing to recognize the needs and desires of your mate is a demonstration of insensitivity. True as this may be, if you recognize needs but fail to respond appropriately to them, you are just as guilty of marital insensitivity. You only have to fail to do one or the other. This is why the following two observations of hypothetical husbands are both accurate.

"He is so insensitive that he wouldn't know a need if it bit him!"

"He is so insensitive that, even though he knows how much I need his help in caring for the kids, he wouldn't lift a finger if my life depended upon it!"

Both of these statements accurately describe instances of insensitivity. Yet, both describe distinctly different aspects of the problem. In the first case, the husband's failure is one of recognition. In the other, his failure is one of response. To the frustrated wives, however, both husbands are transmitting the same message: "I don't care about you!"

Distinguishing between sensitivity and insensitivity is a step in the right direction, but it by no means is a sufficient place to end. Rather, these definitions are the foundation upon which to build a clearer understanding. Insensitivity is a notable adversary. To begin to curtail its power and influence within a relationship, we must far more accurately identify the many forms in which it can appear.

71

Variations

The chart on page 73 summarizes the common variations of sensitivity and insensitivity which I find demonstrated in marriages. It may be helpful to occasionally refer to it for clarification. The chart graphically determines the presence or absence of sensitivity within a relationship by assessing whether recognition and/or response is present. I have found using such a chart to be quite helpful in enhancing understanding.

"Recognition" is placed across the top of the chart and "Response" is placed down the side. Each of these two elements comprising sensitivity are then divided into two sections, Yes and No. Recognition is either present (Yes) or it is absent (No). Response is either present (Yes) or it is absent (No). This division creates a grid with four squares or categories.

All possible options for sensitivity and insensitivity are found within these four categories. Actually, all of the possible options are found within *three* of these categories. The category in the upper right-hand corner of the grid represents impossible options. For example, it would be impossible with our definition of sensitivity for a husband who is failing to recognize the needs and desires of his wife to then respond to them. But the remaining three categories do accurately include all possible variations of sensitivity and insensitivity.

Even though all possible variations of sensitivity and insensitivity are contained in these three categories, I have chosen to describe only the three most common variations within each. Before we look at each variation in detail, there is a point of clarification which I need to make. These are descriptions of how mates tend to behave *most* of the time. They do not necessarily describe how they will behave *all* of the time. Not one of us is *totally* one of these variations or the other. For example, you will not be *totally* genuine and your mate will not be *totally* selfish. Instead, both of you will

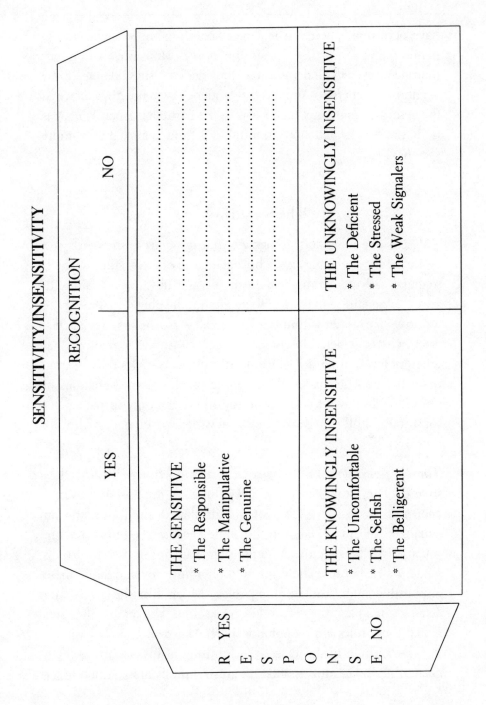

SENSITIVITY/INSENSITIVITY

RECOGNITION

YES

NO

THE SENSITIVE
* The Responsible
* The Manipulative
* The Genuine

THE UNKNOWINGLY INSENSITIVE
* The Deficient
* The Stressed
* The Weak Signalers

THE KNOWINGLY INSENSITIVE
* The Uncomfortable
* The Selfish
* The Belligerent

R YES
E
S
P
O
N
S NO
E

73

have occasions when you will be uncomfortable, or deficient, or manipulative, or. . . . This is the norm. However, within our marriages, we will all demonstrate the characteristics of one of these variations *most often*. And it is this tendency to frequently behave in the described manner which earns us the particular label. With this understanding of variations in mind, it is time to look at these more specifically.

The Sensitive Mate

A sensitive mate both recognizes *and* responds to the needs and desires of his or her partner. The blatant and obvious failures which so graphically define insensitivity are notably absent. The failure to see . . . the failure to do . . . these are not the characteristics of the sensitive. Yet, even within this broad category, there are characteristics which, when closely examined, cause us to realize that different levels of sensitivity can be distinguished. Much like gazing upon the varying shades of any primary color, some variations of sensitivity display a true red whereas others can only manage paler substitutes. Following are shades or variations of mates who are sensitive.

The Responsible.   Responsible mates do things because they should. They want to do the right thing. A responsible husband cooperates with his wife's requests for shared child care and an equalized division of labor in the home because good husbands are supposed to be helpful. A responsible wife meets her husband's sexual needs because she wants to do her duty. By and large, these responsible mates are fulfilling roles. Much like the actors and actresses in a play, they are following a script. The major difference is that these roles are monotonously reenacted on a daily basis.

A responsible husband sees the fulfilling of his role as "doing a good job." In fact, this is often his greatest motivation. Much of his marital ego is tied to his ability to do the honorable thing. Being basically a nice guy, it is important to maintain the responsible image. This responsible nature may even be the high point of the relationship for him. No one could ever accuse him of shirking his husbandly duty . . . or could they?

Obviously missing from this variation is the emotional element. Its absence is noted in two ways. First, as suggested above, mates do things because they ought to and not because they want to. They go to great extremes to do the responsible thing but seldom are they motivated by any sense of true emotional caring.

The second manner in which the absence of emotion is noted is in the *selective* nature of responsible sensitivity. In reality, a responsible mate is being truly sensitive to only *some* of his partner's needs. With the absence of an emotional quality, most of the giving centers around tasks and family maintenance needs. The mundane demands and physical needs required for the normal functioning of the home are the issues which are responded to with sensitivity. The affectional and emotional needs of valuing, esteeming, supporting, affirming, etc., are largely neglected. Obviously missing are sincere hugs, times of individual and interested listening, and spontaneously seized opportunities for reassurance and support.

Pam and James provide us with an example of this form of sensitivity. Pam came for counseling because she was extremely frustrated with her marriage. More specifically, she was frustrated with James. She complained that she was about to lose her mind over an apparent contradiction in her husband.

On the one hand, I don't get what I want from James. I don't get a kiss unless I kiss him. We set speed records when we make love and he seldom initiates any conversation. Yet, on the other hand, he's very cooperative. He does his fair share around the house, always brings his paycheck home for me to manage the family finances, and willingly does about anything I ask him. I trust him completely and don't think he would ever violate our marriage, yet I find the contradiction between pleasing me in some areas and not pleasing me in others to be extremely frustrating.

James is no contradiction . . . only *responsible*. He easily demonstrates sensitivity around the mundane demands of married life because that is the responsible thing to do. The emotional element—the demonstration of real caring—is not the responsible thing to do. Unfortunately for James, Pam knows the difference. Unfortunately for the marriage, *the* difference makes *a* difference.

The Manipulative.   *Manipulation* is a harsh term. When used as a descriptor, it usually prompts negative feelings and connotations. This being the case, you may wonder how I can use manipulative as a description of a variation of sensitivity. It is really not difficult. Some mates are simply manipulatively sensitive.

Manipulative mates do recognize and respond to the needs and desires of their partners. However, their sensitivity is *inconsistent*. There are times when they are more recognizing and more responding than other times. Manipulative mates are more sensitive when being so benefits them the most. They play a game commonly referred to as "Tit for Tat." In professional circles, we would use terms like "compensatory behavior" and "bargaining" to refer to this game. But regardless of the specific term used, the meaning is the same. The manipulatively sensitive mate responds to the needs of a spouse because he desires something in return. To state it simply, he expects a payoff.

Motivation due to an anticipated payoff is the primary characteristic of this form of sensitivity. Unlike the responsible mate, there is nothing honorable here. You husbands, have you ever been guilty of bringing your wife flowers with the real motivation being one of easing your way toward a hunting trip? Or, have you ever taken your wife out to dinner as a bargaining chip for an upcoming golfing weekend? You wives, have you ever been inordinately "affectionate" with the intended goal being to lessen the resistance to the purchase of a new dress or coat? These are all examples of manipulative behavior.

Manipulative behavior, however, exceeds the special events like those described above. It also characterizes the day-to-day exchanges. A manipulative husband will be more polite and more interested than usual in what his wife has to say when he wants to make love that night. A manipulative wife will be extra nice when she wants her husband to watch the children for an evening. Are you getting a feel for the manipulative form of sensitivity? Event by event, day by day, the bartering proceeds. "You have something that I want. What do you want in exchange?"

When both mates practice this form of sensitivity, the marriage takes on a very businesslike appearance. The bartering becomes more open and up front. There is an attitude of "we both know what is going on so let's get down to business." Sometimes the relationship even degenerates to an even-the-score scenario. You are going hunting so your wife is going on a weekend shopping spree with her girlfriends in order to equal things out. This even-the-score scenario was not present at the beginning of your marriage. But over the years of travel, it is a destination at which your relationship has arrived. You are now merely omitting some of the former niceties and formalities.

Eventually, manipulative sensitivity is seen for what it is. The tendency of always looking for a payoff, always having an ulterior motive, and always being inconsistently sensitive, becomes alarmingly apparent. With the realization of emotional dishonesty, relational deterioration escalates. The years of being tricked, used, and conned may even result in the development of heavy resentment. Weary and resistant, even greater emotional distance enters your relationship. You drift. So goes the fate of manipulative sensitivity.

The Genuine. It is easier to describe this variation of sensitivity having already identified its lesser substitutes. A genuine husband behaves responsibly and does what he is supposed to do, but not because he is supposed to do it. A genuine wife is nice to her husband and is fully aware of the benefits of being so, but her attentive and responsive behavior is not motivated by any anticipated payoff. Rather, each is sensitive to the needs of the respective mate because each genuinely cares.

In love, he wants to be all he can be to his wife. With pleasure, she values the opportunities for closeness presented by his needing her. With sensitivity, he genuinely affirms her worth as a person. With cooperation, she demonstrates her appreciation for him as a mate. Quite obviously, all of this is in sharp contrast to the behavior of the responsible and the manipulative.

The genuine husband has mastered the giving issue within the relationship. Somehow he has resolved how to balance the extremes of being either *too* giving or *not* giving enough. He recognizes that he cannot, and realistically should not, meet all of his wife's needs. He has learned to appropriately discriminate between that which is excessive and that which is legitimate. Wisely, he recognizes that sometimes the most sensitive response is one which is contradictory to his wife's expectations.

Likewise, the genuine wife has also mastered this balance. She allows her husband to be responsible where he needs to be . . . and she expects the same in return. On a continuum with the two end points of oversensitivity and insensitivity being pushed to extremes, she finds herself somewhere in the middle. With a genuinely sensitive stance, she responds in a manner which is consistently in his best interest.

Sensing his wife's needs, and deeply caring, a genuinely sensitive husband always responds. Even when his response is neither the desired nor the expected, he never simply ignores or discounts. He cares too much for both his wife and the relationship to do that.

Valuing his mate, as well as her ability to be responsible, he responds. Sensing his truly caring attitude and respect, she responds. Together, a relationship is built.

Genuinely sensitive mates seem to be in the minority. If this were not the case, we would find the incidence of marital failure to be somewhat less than is currently being experienced. Possibly the problem is one of improper connection. Maybe genuine people are failing to marry other genuine people. Although some of this does occur, I strongly suspect that much of the problem rests with the changeable nature of relationships. Many mates probably enter marriage fairly representative of a genuine mate. Somehow, over the years, they progressively evolve into a far lesser substitute. As their level of sensitivity begins to change, so does the relationship. They begin to drift. Without genuine sensitivity, a truly successful marriage is impossible to achieve.

The Knowingly Insensitive Mate

The knowingly insensitive mate has no difficulty recognizing the needs and desires of his marital partner. He knows what they are. He simply fails to respond to them. As a receptor, he is fine. As a responder, he is not so fine. But, as with the other categories, knowingly insensitive mates are not all alike. Within this category, there are characteristics which allow us to identify three distinctly different groupings such as the uncomfortable, the selfish, and the belligerent.

The Uncomfortable. Ben and Dorothy came for counseling after 26 years of marriage. Things between them had never been great, but at least they had been tolerable, that is, until about five years ago. It was then that their youngest son entered college. As Ben and Dorothy's youngest child began to be physically absent from the home, the emotional distance which so characterized their marriage became extremely apparent. The secret was out. Ben and Dorothy both recognized that their marriage had been drifting.

How did they respond to this realization? Ben responded to the change brought by their son's absence by throwing himself more into his work. He managed to be gone more hours a day and traveled more days a week. From his perspective, this was a workable solution that obviously did nothing toward improving the marriage but it did alleviate the immediate crisis.

With her children and husband both gone, Dorothy dealt with the isolation by investing more of her spare time and energy into clubs and social activities. The crisis had been averted but an unexpected change in Ben's job occurred. With the change came a new routine and he was no longer forced to travel. Forced to be alone together, at the same place and at the same time, Ben and Dorothy found the tension to be unbearable. It was not unusual for days to go by without an unnecessary word being said. They were seemingly locked into distant positions and found themselves incapable of breaking the grip which this had on their relationship. Finally, with tension at a maximum level, an explosion occurred resulting in a separation. In the midst of this crisis, it was decided that counseling might be helpful.

In the first session the true scenario began to unfold. The recounting of the hurts and frustrations of twenty-six years of marriage began to shed light on what was happening in the present. In the early years of their relationship, Dorothy had repeatedly tried to draw close to Ben. She would share with him some of her deepest feelings and talk to him of her needs for emotional closeness. Ben responded only with silence or further distancing. In frustration, Dorothy began to emotionally back away from Ben and found her children to be suitable preoccupations—until they went off to college.

How did Ben allow this to happen? Was he really aware of Dorothy's needs in the earlier years of marriage? Did he truly care for her? Did he not really desire a closer and more intimate relationship himself? To all of these questions, Ben responded in the affirmative. He was aware . . . he did care . . . and he did desire a closer relationship. Then where was the problem? Where did things go wrong? Simply stated, drawing close to someone was a very difficult endeavor for Ben. Emotional closeness was scary. As Ben indicated in the session:

> I've always just "stuffed things in." Not only in the
> marriage, but with others as well. I can't share anything.
> Listening is a little easier. But when it comes to responding,
> I just freeze up. It's not that I don't want to. I just can't.

Although clearly recognizing Dorothy's needs, Ben failed to respond to them. His insensitivity was neither a lack of caring nor a difference in desire. But regardless of intent or desire, he knowingly failed to respond because to do otherwise was, for him, extremely *uncomfortable*.

Another couple with whom I have worked, Cleve and Joan, came for counseling after only three years of marriage. Their story was very similar to the early years of Ben and Dorothy but they had not yet moved to extremely distant positions or developed outside preoccupations. However, they recognized the potential for doing so, and this scared them. They had discussed where each thought their marriage would be in five years, ten years, and fifteen years if they did not change what was happening. They questioned whether their marriage would even "be" in fifteen years.

The observations and complaints were similar to Ben and Dorothy's. Within the relationship, Joan shared and Cleve did not. Both cared deeply for one another and desired an intimate relationship. Yet, both seemed to be frustrated by their failure to progress toward this goal. The difference between them and Ben and Dorothy was in Cleve's perspective as to *why* he failed to respond to Joan's emotional needs:

> I know what she wants from me. I just don't know *how* to do
> it. I don't know how to respond to her . . . how to reach out
> . . . how to share what is really a part of me.

Whereas Ben's discomfort came from the thoughts of drawing close to his wife and sharing himself with her, Cleve claimed that his discomfort came from his ignorance of **how to** appropriately respond to his wife. Sometimes I wonder how much true difference exists between these two complaints. I am not saying that they are synonymous, but there is probably a great deal of overlapping in the two. What is clear, however, is that the anxiety and discomfort produced in either instance prompts the affected mate to knowingly disregard the needs of his spouse.

Ben responded to Dorothy's overtures for closeness with silence and withdrawal. Cleve responded in much the same manner toward Joan. In essence, their nonresponse was a response. And with repeated occurrences, what began as isolated reactions of frustration and anger on the part of Dorothy and Joan gradually evolved into persistent and constantly present attitudes of resentment and resistance. Coldness began to permeate their relationships.

Without a change in the demonstrated level of sensitivity, the distance being experienced in Cleve and Joan's marriage will become as firmly entrenched as it is in Ben and Dorothy's. Without intervention, their marriage will in all likelihood deteriorate and may drift along for years, but without change it will fail.

The Selfish.   If there is one statement that most appropriately describes the main characteristic of the selfish, it is this: "My needs and desires are far more important to me than are yours." That simple statement says it all. The selfish mate does what he wants regardless of the needs and desires of his mate.

How about spending some time with the children? "No, I'm too busy." How about giving up a golfing weekend to spend time with the wife? "No, I like to play golf." How about listening to some of the wife's concerns? "No, I have no interest in that kind of stuff." How about giving up some of your social activities and preoccupations with the children to spend some quality time with the husband? "No, these activities are important to me." How about staying within the family budget instead of constantly replenishing the wardrobe? "No, I like new clothes." Selfish mates know what they like and what they do not like. What they like is to be able to do exactly what they want when they want. What they do not like is any demand made upon them. In short, they resent any form of restriction.

Although selfish mates are similar in regard to their intent to do as they please, their expectations for the behavior of their own spouses may differ. Some selfish mates do as they please and expect very little difference in return from their spouse. "I'll do as I please and you can do the same." Others, on the other hand, while rejecting any form of personal obligation to the marriage, are highly demanding of their mates. It is a sad bit of irony which finds a selfish mate to be both very rejecting of any demands being placed upon him, while at the same time, excessively demanding of those around him. This latter form of selfishness is probably the most difficult to deal with.

Selfish mates are really motivated by only one thing—the satisfaction of self. Their own needs are all-important. Everyone else can take a backseat. Sometimes their true motivations are masked by worthy causes. All-out efforts toward noble goals are cited as rationales for failing to respond to marital needs. But alas, for the selfish, these are only feeble attempts at justifying insensitivity. If the truth were known, their true goals are not the honorable causes to which they pledge allegiance, but rather are their own self-satisfying needs for power, success, achievement, glory, recognition, etc. These truer goals taint any achievement they may ultimately attain.

It has always amazed me how some mates will successfully pursue a noble cause only to leave a devastated marriage and family in the wake . . . and all of this at the applause and admiration of the masses. There seems to be some grave inconsistency here.

Wives who want to be genuine have a difficult time remaining so with selfish husbands. After repeated incidents of being discounted, rejected, and taken for granted, the insensitivity takes its toll. Having given much and received little in return, the genuine wife gradually moves to another variation. Possibly she becomes responsible and, at least, does her duty. Perhaps she will become manipulative and bargain for a better share of things. The most conflictual pairings seem to be when both mates are selfish and excessively demanding of each other.

I once counseled with a couple who were both selfish. They were "takers," totally unwilling to "give" to each other within the relationship. Even though they felt very little personal obligation toward giving, each expected a great deal from the other. With two selfish mates within the same relationship, conflict was predictable and after 15 years of constant harrassment, they divorced. Both of them were in poor health, emotionally and physically. Their respective insensitivity had definitely taken its toll.

Regardless of the specific match-up, things do not go well for selfish mates within marriage. The marriage may survive the years of friction, but the relationship does not. Even if the poorly matched mate discovers a means for tolerating the insanity of this marriage, it will be merely that—toleration. Marriages endured with selfishness can *optimally* expect to be only *minimally* rewarding.

The Belligerent.   Belligerent mates are angry mates and the person with whom they are angry is their spouse. All of their other interpersonal involvements may be quite amiable. In fact, those who are involved with the belligerent husband or wife in other relationships might possibly be shocked or surprised were they to witness what often occurs in the home. Away from the home and mate, there may be little to suggest that anything but a normal home life exists. But in the home, the battle rages. It requires only a brief amount of time in the presence of a belligerent couple for the underlying tension to become apparent.

There are some aspects of the belligerent form of insensitivity which make it uniquely different from other variations. The most differentiating of these aspects is its *cooperative* nature. Whereas most of the other variations are descriptions of how individuals respond within a marriage, belligerent is most often descriptive of the couple. If the belligerent form of insensitivity is present in a relationship, it is generally being exhibited by both mates.

In part, the demonstration of this form of insensitivity by both mates is what maintains or perpetuates its presence. They appear to be helplessly locked into a battle, with neither one able to change the style of interaction. Caught in a web of intense emotions, the belligerent form of insensitivity is continued.

Other factors which differentiate the belligerent form of insensitivity from other variations are (1) intention and (2) intensity. Although all forms of the knowingly insensitive have mates who deliberately fail to respond to the needs and desires of their marital partners, belligerent mates do so with excessive intent. They are angry. With extreme determination, they absolutely refuse to respond in a positive way. Their intention to be insensitive is far more deliberate than that of other variations. Second, this deliberate and decisive failure to respond is generally extremely emotion laden. Belligerent insensitivity always carries with it an element of intense emotion.

Belligerent couples are motivated by a quest for power within the relationship. They are locked in a power struggle. Belligerent acts are aimed at either controlling the mate or resisting control by the mate. These acts are commonly demonstrated in the form of:

1. *Resistance* "No, I won't."
2. *Defiance* "I'll do it anyway."
3. *Challenge* "I dare you."
4. *Retaliation* "I'm getting even."
5. *Noncooperation* "Whatever you want, the answer is NO."

Sometimes these belligerent actions are demonstrated openly and obviously. At other times, they emerge in a far more subtle or passive form. For example, a wife who intends to resist her husband's requests in regard to having clean shirts for work may either openly refuse to do them ("I'm tired of washing your shirts. If you want clean shirts, do them yourself!") or she can passively resist by forgetting to do them. In either case, she is responding belligerently.

In the example just cited, it's not the wife's refusal to do shirts that is the real issue. Many wives do not do shirts. The real issue which labels this action as belligerent insensitivity is her reason or motivation for refusing to do her husband's shirts. She is intentionally demonstrating her power within the relationship. "You do not control me. In fact, you have so little power, you can't even get me to do your shirts. So, there!"

I came home from the office one afternoon to be met at the front door by my wife and one of our neighbors. Jan wanted to go somewhere with the neighbor, which would require some adjustments in my schedule. After briefly discussing the situation, it was cooperatively resolved. Observing the entire dialogue, our neighbor friend commented: "That seemed so easy." Actually, it was easy. It's not difficult to be cooperative when both mates value each other's needs as significantly as they value their own. But to our neighbor, who was locked into a belligerent power struggle with her husband, cooperation was a rare commodity. They could not resolve even a problem as simple as this was. Cooperation can be easy. But when you are locked into a power struggle, nothing is easy.

It has always amused me to observe the great extent to which belligerent mates will go in order to appear rational or right. This is frequently the case when they come in for counseling. If I were to allow it to continue, I could sit for hours and listen to one rational explanation after another aimed at justifying why a husband has taken an opposite position from that of his wife over issue after issue. In actuality, both have plausible rationales; however, neither is speaking the truth. Neither position may be any more right than the other. But their motivation is not rightness, it is power. They are resisting each other. Pushed to extremes, they absolutely refuse to cooperate with one another. For belligerent couples, this form of behavior is the norm. Unless this manner of relating changes, the relationship only continues to deteriorate.

The Unknowingly Insensitive Mate

An unknowingly insensitive mate fails to recognize the needs and desires of his spouse. Because he fails to perceive, he undoubtedly fails to respond. Whether he would respond, even if he were aware, is not known. What is known, however, is that by failing to recognize the needs of his mate, he will never get the chance to respond to them. You cannot respond to what you do not recognize. As with the variations of the sensitive and the knowingly insensitive, those within this category also differ greatly. Three common variations (the deficient, the stressed, and the weak signalers) and the characteristics which distinguish them are described below.

The Deficient. The term *deficient* is defined as "lacking in some necessary quality or element." It implies that something is defective. In a very real sense, deficient mates are defective. They lack a very vital interpersonal quality. They lack the capacity to perceive the needs of others.

Sometimes this deficiency emerges in the form of psychological blindness, meaning that some mates are simply oblivious to the interpersonal world around them. They may have an exceptional knowledge of computers. They may have a superior grasp of the laws of basic and nuclear physics. They may even be wizards at solving Rubik's Cubes. But amidst all of these apparent capabilities, they lack one crucial interpersonal element—the ability to perceive the needs of others. As you might guess, this perceptual inadequacy has definite ramifications for a marriage.

Jim and Carol had been married for 6 years. When they came for counseling, Jim was upset and scared. Carol was extremely angry. Jim's panicked condition was the result of Carol's announcement that she wanted a divorce. Carol's anger and announcement were the result of six years of insensitivity. Jim's true feelings for Carol were quickly identified. Interestingly, although he was perceived as insensitive, he really did care for her. What was even more interesting, however, was Jim's total confusion as to what was going on. He had no idea as to *why* Carol was upset, *how* the marriage had gotten to such a condition as to warrant counseling, or *what* was supposed to happen next. Even in the midst of marital crisis, he could not understand or perceive the needs of his wife.

In the session, Carol spoke to Jim of her desires for quality time together, the mutual sharing of feelings and ideas, and just his bodily presence as an empathetic listener. She complained of his always being in his own little world. She might as well have been speaking in a foreign language. The puzzled look on Jim's face and the long silence when she finished her statements confirmed what I suspected. Jim had a definite deficit. Something was missing. Something was absent. In his frame of reference, these requests did not compute. He couldn't even understand the need for these desires, much less recognize Carol's requests for them.

Recognizing Jim's obvious deficiency, it is not too difficult to understand Carol's frustration. Nor is it difficult to determine **why,** **how,** and **what** is going on. Exactly **where** the relationship will go from here is an altogether different question. Marriages like this can drift for a season, but once a crisis is reached, a change must take place for them to survive.

The Stressed.   Stressed mates are both similar and different when compared to the deficient. The similarity in these two variations is in their common behavior. Like their deficient cohorts, stressed mates also fail to recognize the needs of their mates. They, too, seem to be in their own little world. But after this, the similarity ceases.

The primary difference in these two variations is in the area of motivation. Extreme amounts of external pressure, often due to situations seemingly beyond their control, take their toll on a stressed mate's ability to perceive the needs of others. At another time or place, and given a more positive set of circumstances, they could very possibly respond with an entirely different form of sensitivity. But in their present context, insensitivity is the order of the day.

Stressed mates are typically normal people. They are normal people under extreme pressure. Our society is pressure packed. More and more of us are living in the fast lane. The promise of ease so adamantly heralded by propagators of high technology has failed to materialize. What promised to simplify our existence has only complicated our lives. Although technological advancement has been extremely influential in vocational areas, it is by no means limited to this field. Rarely is any area of life untouched by scientific progress. With exasperation, we often yearn for a return to what was once a simpler style of life.

Sometimes couples are caught in the pressure of unexpected crisis. Sudden illnesses, job changes, deaths in the family, tragic events, etc., by themselves can be problematic. But especially when they are piggybacked with other events, these can stress out a mate and a marriage. A client came to me reporting many symptoms of depression. In checking for a precipitating cause or event, she informed me that her daughter had recently been abused by a neighbor. Further exploration, however, revealed that this problem in reference to her daughter was only the most recent in a long list of events. In fact, in my client's words, it was the last straw. During the five years prior to her coming for counseling, she had experienced (1) the loss of two sisters; (2) a major heart attack which affected both her physical health and her level of activity; (3) severe financial reversal; (4) employment problems; and (5) the assault on her daughter. She felt as though life was beating her down. It probably was. Sadly, as it beat her down it also interfered with her ability to relate to her husband.

As you can see, stress comes in many different forms. It may emerge in the form of constant and long-term pressure as in the case of continued financial stress or, on the other hand, it may suddenly appear as an unforeseen major crisis, like the death of a child. Sometimes it is the result of one event. At other times, it is the composite product of many combined problems which are piggy-backed together. Singularly, they may have been manageable. Together, however, they become overwhelming. Regardless of the fact that stress may come in any one of a number of forms, the result of this stress is still the same. When stressed, mates tend to the more urgent issues. When stressed, mates become insensitive . . . and when mates are insensitive, the relationship begins to drift, placing the marriage at risk.

Weak Signalers.   Weak signalers are significantly different from all of the other variations which I have thus far identified. The other sensitivity forms have been determined by the success or failure of a mate to recognize and respond to the needs of his marital partner. With the weak signaler variation, this failure to recognize a mate's needs is readily acknowledged. However, contrary to other forms, this failure is not the problem. The true problem rests with the failure of his mate to adequately make her needs and desires known. In this instance, the alleged insensitivity is actually a bum rap.

This variation definitely carries with it the flavor of interaction. For instance, while a husband may be disparaged for being uncaring and unfeeling, it is his wife's role which really precipitates this interactional failure. She simply failed to make her needs known. For all we know, the nonresponding husband is being unjustly criticized. He may be more than willing to respond to his partner's needs. Furthermore, he may be more than capable of recognizing these needs when appropriately expressed. But, as the scenario goes:

1. The needs and desires of his wife are not expressed;
2. since they are not expressed, they are not recognized;
3. since they are not recognized, they are not responded to;
4. therefore, in failing to recognize and respond to his wife's needs, the husband is accused of insensitivity.

Actually a victim, he emerges as a culprit.

Weak signalers fail to assume responsibility for making their needs known. When confronted about their own failure, they usually respond with one of three reasons or excuses:

(1) "He ought to know." This is the classic excuse of this variation. Weak signalers commonly make statements like, "If he were really sensitive, if he truly cared, he would know what I need. I shouldn't have to say a thing." Husbands and wives who believe and practice this myth are endorsing the concept of mind reading. They believe that one criterion for being a sensitive mate is the ability to read minds. I think you would agree that this expectation is somewhat excessive.

(2) "It's inappropriate to ask." This is another commonly used excuse for failing to make needs known to a mate. With women, this attitude emerges as a false femininity. "Why, it would be highly unladylike to express needs." They believe that true ladies are pleasant, demure and sweet . . . and to ask for attention is totally unacceptable. With men, the attitude emerges as an extreme machismo. Not only do real men not eat quiche . . . neither do

they express needs. You never heard Rhett Butler or "the Duke" talking about their needs. Neither will these husbands.

(3) "I'm just too easygoing." This is the final commonly used excuse for failing to make needs known to a mate. This phrase is a kind way of describing what is in reality a totally nonproductive behavior. Being too nice or being passive are more accurate descriptions. Passive mates deny their own personal rights. They deny their right to have needs. By so doing, they also deny their right to have them met. Following this line of reasoning, they are just easygoing and settle for what naturally comes their way . . . at least, for a while.

Weak signalers live with a fantasy. What always seems to accompany the excuse for failing to make their needs known is the expectation that somehow their needs will be recognized and all of their dreams fulfilled. This seldom ever happens. What more realistically does happen is that the weak signaler becomes increasingly frustrated and angry. But little of this is directly communicated to the unsuspecting mate . . . at least until it has gotten to such a proportion as to be volatile . . . and then it erupts.

When a weak-signaling wife finally gets fed up and explodes, who do you think gets the blame? You guessed it. The insensitive and uncaring husband. He is blamed, but not at fault. But even though the accusations are false, this does not change the destructive consequences for the relationship. Once again, an inappropriate form of marital interaction has taken its toll on a relationship.

What You Can Do

Evaluate Your Situation

One of the most productive things you can do is to cooperatively complete a thorough sensitivity evaluation. What are the variations of sensitivity demonstrated in your marriage? Who is the more sensitive? Who is the lesser? Is one of you overly sensitive?

This activity is most helpful when 3 steps are followed: assess, compare, and discuss.

1. Assess. Working independently, decide which sensitivity/ insensitivity variation best describes your typical behavior. Write it down on a sheet of paper. After making a selection, prove it. What makes you think you are what you say you are? List these reasons on your sheet of paper, also. After assessing your level of sensitivity, repeat the process for your mate. What do you perceive his or her level of sensitivity to be? Why? Prove it.

2. Compare. Exchange your assessment sheets and allow ample time for thoughtful contemplation. It may be that you will want to set a specific time in the future for discussion prior to actually exchanging these sensitivity assessments. Regardless, it is important to allow enough time for a genuine consideration of your mate's evaluation. How much discrepancy is there between your perception of your behavior and the opinion of your mate? Where does most of the discrepancy lie? Can you understand his or her perspective? Where do you agree? Where do you disagree? Think about it.

3. Discuss. The overriding purpose for completing the assessment and comparison steps is to arrive at this point. The primary goal is to get you constructively talking to one another about what is happening within your marriage. Again, I do not want to lessen the importance of assessment and comparison. These two preparatory steps are crucial to meaningful discussion. All 3 steps (assess, compare, and discuss) are vitally important. To omit any one of these would greatly reduce the effectiveness of this procedure. Couples who fail to evaluate their situation by thorough assessment and comparison often find efforts to discuss extremely futile. What is needed here is for discussion to be more than just the idle sharing of opinions and viewpoints. Truly discuss your findings. What was the sensitivity like when you first married? What is it like now? How would you like for it to be? These are the kinds of questions which need to be discussed. The depth of discussion which follows a thorough self-assessment can be very rewarding.

It may be that this discussion phase will require repeated conversations. Time limitations, intense emotions, confusion, or any number of legitimate problems may interfere with this meaningful experience. Do not be alarmed if this is the situation. Merely commit yourselves to another time of sharing together. It will be time well spent.

Accept Responsibility

The Evaluation Exercise is a conjoint activity. In other words, it requires the participation of both you and your mate. The suggestion of accepting responsibility, on the other hand, is directed to each of you as individuals. It should be accomplished independent of the efforts of your spouse and regardless of his behavior. In reference to sensitivity, then, there are two ways in which you need to accept personal responsibility:

1. Make your needs known.   Avoid being a weak signaler. Although you cannot control how your mate responds to your needs, you can at least take responsibility for his being aware of them. This is best accomplished with a pleasant and direct approach. An honest sharing of concerns, needs, and wishes seems to evoke the least amount of defensiveness and has the best assurance that you are being heard. The two approaches to absolutely avoid are (a) direct attacks and (b) "hinting," neither of which is a productive way to express needs. For example, if you wanted to spend more time with your mate, there are a number of ways in which you could handle this situation. You could attack him and say something like this:

You never spend any time with me. All you care about are your own interests.

You could hint around about your desire to spend more time with your mate by saying something like this:

According to the weather report, next weekend is going to be gorgeous. Remember how we used to go on picnics when the weather was nice?

Or, you could use what we commonly refer to as "I statements." These are direct and honest statements, which express what you feel, believe, desire, etc. An example of a direct statement in this situation would be:

I have a need to spend more time with you. Why don't we look at our schedules and make some plans.

Direct and emotionally honest expressions leave little opportunity for your signal to be weak. Furthermore, the absence of a direct attack on your mate lessens the possibility of a defensive reaction. All in all, this approach offers you the best opportunity for getting what you want . . . greater sensitivity in your mate.

2. Change your own level of sensitivity.   Again, you are not responsible for what your mate does. However, you are responsible for what *you* do. If you are not satisfied with your level of sensitivity within the marriage, change it. All variations are changeable. We have already discussed how some insensitive mates did not enter marriage with that form of behavior. Over the years their level of sensitivity declined. The opposite can occur. If you really want more out of your marriage, you will have to begin by taking responsibility for yourself. What stops you from being more sensitive? Deal with it! You *can* take control of your situation.

— 6 —
THE CARES OF THIS LIFE

I was present in a Sunday-school class recently where the teacher was presenting a lesson about the trials encountered by Jesus in His forty-day wilderness experience. The class members thoroughly discussed the differences among the three attacks launched by Satan and how Jesus dealt with each one. It was the teacher's intention to make a creative leap from the emphasis on the trials faced by Jesus to those faced by each of us as we attempt to nurture our Christian experience.

I found it rather revealing that no one seemed to be willing to give much positive credit to the trials and crises encountered in life. For the most part, trials were seen as painful. There was a fear that crises could be overwhelming. The shock of a sudden impact—the anxiety accompanying having to give someone or something up—the insecurity of change—all of these demands could prove to be too much to handle. From the collective vantage point of the class, crisis events were labeled as adversaries to spiritual growth and maturity and were dreaded.

After a few moments of thought, I challenged this line of reasoning. I asked the teacher and the other class members, "What do you do when you are faced with a crisis? How do you respond?" After a brief period of silence, spontaneous responses of "Pray more," "Try to draw closer to the Lord," "Spend more time in His Word," began to echo throughout the classroom. I then asked another question: "What is the result of these responses to crises?" Obviously, the answers to this question were more than "one liners." But one by one, class members began to testify of the faithfulness of God to His people. In short, as they began to pray, to seek, and to search the Scriptures, they began to gain a "peace which passeth understanding" and, ultimately, a faith that was even more vibrant and resilient than before the crisis event. With this as a result, it was difficult for me to totally identify trials and crises as adversaries.

Basically, the process of faith is the process of God's intervention in our lives. We truly get to know Him through His interventions. We can *hear* about His works; we can *read* about His majesty; we can even *theorize* about His existence; but we only truly learn to *love* Him as we experience Him in our lives. As a good friend once told me, "We are all faced with a series of opportunities brilliantly disguised as impossible situations." Faced with these seemingly impossible situations, the integrity of our faith is challenged. As we seek the Lord and, in return, as He intervenes in our distress, His formula for spiritual maturation is revealed. Like the gold which passes through the assayer's fire, we too are purified (see 1 Peter 1:7).

This probably would have been a good place for the class to have ended. Most of the members were feeling encouraged in reference to facing any upcoming trials. However, I believed there was a need to press the point a little further. It was not enough to merely gain consensus that, even though unpleasant, God's design for spiritual growth often includes trials. I felt it was still important to go on and identify an adversary. If trials and crises are not necessarily counterproductive to our Christian walk, could we identify something that is a true adversary?

I must admit that this entire line of thought did not spontaneously occur to me on that particular Sunday morning. For several weeks prior to this class, I had been taking stock of my own spiritual inward journey. The weeks of introspection had resulted in the identification of three predominant circumstantial themes throughout the majority of my adult life. First, there is the theme of *crisis*. These are the times of turmoil . . . at least, initial turmoil. They are the "unexpecteds" of life. They are the things for which I am not prepared. They catch me off guard. I am surprised. But they are a vehicle which draws me closer to God. After time, stability is regained and victory is reported.

The second theme is one of *calmness*. These are the times in my life when everything is at peace. There are no major demands being made upon me . . . no rigid schedules . . . no excessive expectations. In these calm periods of my life, time is definitely within my control. The Lord is consciously in the center of my day. There is always ample time and opportunity for prayer, Bible reading, and meditation upon His goodness. Truly, these are my best days. Everything is right with the world and my relationship with the Lord seems to become more intimate. From this vantage point, it is easy to see why I perceive this a major asset to my inward journey.

The final theme in my life is one of *hecticness*. Unlike the periods of calm, there is very little peace during these times. Demands abound . . . schedules are full . . . expectations are high. There is never enough time to get everything done and what time there is seems to be beyond my control. I desire for the Lord to be at the center of my day, but after all is said and done, He seems to get lost in the shuffle. Pray in the car . . . meditate on the run . . . read tomorrow.

Truly, these are my worst days. Whereas periods of crisis and calmness serve to draw me closer to God, hecticness pulls me away. It is my adversary. Little by little, it subtly robs me of the closeness of my relationship with the Lord. It is the major threat to my inward journey.

The other members in the class seemed to identify with what I was sharing. They too had experienced these three periods in their lives. And even though their responses may have been somewhat different during these times, they could not deny the reality or the impact of their presence.

Now, it has not been my intention to teach a Sunday-school lesson or to give an exegesis in practical theology. Rather, I am endeavoring to provide a metaphor or analogy to be used as a comparison to our marital relationships. Just as in our spiritual lives, marriages will intermittently move from one of these three themes to another. There will be times of crisis . . . there will be times of calmness . . . there will be times of hecticness. And our marriages respond to each of these three themes in different ways. In the times of crisis, a marriage may be threatened by unexpected external events which can level severe barrages of pressure upon a relationship. But, similar to the crises experienced in our spiritual walk, these crises can also work for the good of the marriage. You can emerge stronger, healthier, and even more resolutely committed to one another. In the times of calmness, marriages can grow. At least, the potential for growth is present. It is easier in periods of calmness to attend to the marriage. Less effort is required to find time for one another. Those things which compete for our attention are reduced. Schedules are lighter. Demands are fewer. Truly, everything is easier.

Although these are the times which should be seized and capitalized upon, frequently they are not. Sometimes, through drifting, mates have become so emotionally disconnected from each other that there is little motivation to utilize these infrequent boons to the marital life-style. In fact, it is possible for periods of calm to even threaten a marriage. In the silence of the calm, a mate may become painfully aware of the absence of any true intimacy in the relationship. Although this sudden awareness allows for the opportunity of corrective measures, some mates fail to do what they "need" to do, and only become more disgruntled with their marriage. It is almost ironic. This period of time seems to offer a great deal of potential for the enhancement of a marriage. Yet, oftentimes, couples will fail to seize the opportunity to capitalize on this resource.

In both times of crisis and calmness, there is at least the potential for good. In times of hecticness, however, the potential for growth is absent. Marriages suffer during this time . . . sometimes to disastrous proportions. From the vantage point of marital relationships, the characteristics accompanying hectic life-styles are dangerous. So maritally speaking, hecticness is our adversary. And part of its most dangerous potential rests with its contribution toward drifting.

Hecticness: A Case of Double Normality

Much of our difficulty in dealing with hecticness revolves around a problem I call double normality. First of all, hecticness is a problem for *normal people*. It is a problem of the ordinary and not just the exceptional . . . whether exceptionally good or exceptionally bad. You do not have to be exceptionally bright, exceptionally talented, or exceptionally industrious . . . although you may be. Neither do you have to be exceptionally inept, exceptionally undisciplined, or exceptionally disorganized . . . although you may be. It is not just a problem for company executives, business owners, or professionals. It is also a problem for draftsmen, mechanics, and secretaries. It is a problem for all of us . . . all of us normal and ordinary people with normal and ordinary lives. And from normal and ordinary marriages, hecticness claims its victims.

Second, hecticness is a problem of *normal occurrence*. Not only does it plague normal people, it is also normal for hecticness to occur. Its occurrence is predictable . . . you can count on it. Although hecticness has long been with us, modern society has only increased its prevalence. Every aspect of our daily life has a quickened pace from that which existed a generation ago. As a nation, we are more industrialized and automated. As a people, we are more mobile and transient. Our homes are convenient and computerized. With all of this progress, I have only one question: If things are so good, why am I so stressed out?

With all this change, why don't we have any more unusurped time? I do not think I would really ever want to return to the simpler life-style of years gone by. I am probably too much a product of this current generation to truly enjoy anything else. However, the thought is occasionally quite tempting. There is no denying that our predecessors lived a simpler life.

The problem of the increased occurrence of hecticness is compounded by another current influence . . . our changing perspective of marriage. The quickened pace of today's society would not nearly so impact upon the marital relationship if we still held to the traditional expectations. In the past, marriage was viewed as an institution which served many perfunctory functions. It was convenient. Emphasis was placed upon rigid roles and everyone doing his duty. The husbandly responsibilities focused around his fulfilling the roles of breadwinner (provider) and head of the home (authority). The wifely responsibilities revolved around the home, including child care (nurturing) and housework. Mutuality, emotional support, demonstrated caring, romance . . . these were low-priority items compared with fulfilling the everyday functional demands.

Far different are the expectations for marriage today. If traditional expectations were still in force, the increase in hecticness would not be nearly so devastating. However, with expectations for intimacy, togetherness, and companionship, the effects of a fast-paced existence are even more impacting. We want more from our marriages today . . . at least, we want more emotionally. Hecticness prevents us from getting what we want.

Hecticness is a product of this age, oftentimes forced upon us, becoming the norm. Be this as it may, to place the blame totally on external circumstances, thus denying any personal responsibility, would be an error. To some extent we must share the blame for the existence of hecticness within our lives and, therefore, for the toll it claims. For you see, what often precipitates and then helps to maintain our adversary is our own overconcern for "the cares of this life."

Far too often, we have a heightened sense of attention for things which really deserve less priority in our lives. This is not to say that having concerns for the cares of this life are necessarily bad. However, when our concerns become excessive, our adversary subtly claims more and more of our energies. In a state of physical, mental, and emotional exhaustion, our marriages drift into bankruptcy.

Why Do We Let It Happen?

What is our motivation? How do we help complicate our lives? As we will see, there is more than one way for us to contribute to our problem.

Family Security

Sometimes hecticness comes in the form of an overconcern for family security. John and Toni came for counseling while already in the process of divorce. They had been separated for three months and this seemed to be their last attempt at halting the proceedings. John was anxious and somewhat despondent. Toni was also anxious, but seemed more emotionally removed from all that was taking place. John wanted the two of them to stay together and viewed counseling as an aid to this end. Toni, on the other hand, was largely present due to John's insistence that they "get help before it's too late." It took only 60 minutes for the two of them to describe a scenario which required twenty years to unfold.

They married at a young age and were initially quite content. After a couple of years, the first of their three children was born. In an effort to provide the standard of living which both of them desired, John took on a second job. As time went by, Toni began to notice how little contact she and John had with one another. She questioned whether a second job was really a necessity. John casually dismissed her concern and continued to pull a double load. Toni resigned herself to the inevitability of John's absence and invested her time and energies into the lives of her children. As a couple, John and Toni began to drift.

During their twenty years of marriage, they were able to achieve their primary goal . . . that of security for the family. They had all of the tangible trappings: a nice house, two cars, financial stability, and lots of extras for the children. They appeared to have everything . . . but they didn't. Suddenly, Toni realized how little they actually did have. And with this realization came the desire to dissolve the marriage.

John used the counseling session as an opportunity to both confess and repent:

> I know that throwing myself into my work the way I did was wrong. I accept full blame for what has happened. But I can change. I want Toni and me to stay together. I want my marriage and I want my family. We can make it work. My only defense is that everything I did was for my family.

Was John a bad person? Were his motives impure? No, he was just overconcerned with the cares of this life. But what were the results? His preoccupation with providing a good standard of living for his children left him little time to get to know them. Although living in the same household, to John, his children were virtual strangers. Obsessed with the cares of life, John lost contact with his wife. In assessing the results, I question whether financial security was really worth the cost.

Personal Achievement

Another way in which we contribute to the hecticness in our lives is to have an excessive desire for personal achievement. Most of us want to be achievers . . . to be good at something. For some of us, it is the recognition of a job well done at work. For others, it may be recreational accomplishments—par golf, twenty-five-pound bass, or 10K runs in less than thirty-two minutes. We each identify our own targets and simultaneously determine what is the acceptable level of achievement to strive for. For some of us, personal achievement is fairly within our grasp. For others, regardless of the accomplishment, it remains just out of reach. Never satisfied, never content, what has been accomplished is never enough. We are driven to achieve higher, to accumulate more, and to do better.

The need to achieve is inbred in our children. Our culture demands it. From their earliest moments, children are encouraged to do their best. Even before entering school they are taught to win and, with winning, to obtain approval. School merely reinforces what they have already come to realize . . . that life is a series of competitive events. Constantly, they are tested, measured, and evaluated. How are they progressing? How do they compare to others? How do they measure up? By the time adulthood is reached, achievement is second nature.

As adults, we are always climbing the proverbial ladder and looking to get ahead. Even television commercials tell us to "be all that you can be," although I do not know if joining the army is necessarily the solution. Be a success. Get to the top. Win. Bigger, better, more . . . these are our strivings.

Yet, our problem is not with achievement in and of itself. Achievement is good. Success is admirable. And winning certainly beats losing. Rather, our real problem is with the excessive need for achievement. Some of us become so obsessed with the need for personal achievement that the pursuit of it causes all other areas of life to sink back into the shadows . . . including our marriage. When this occurs, the need is excessive.

A husband who is excessively oriented toward achievement may repeatedly take on extra responsibilities at work in an effort to get ahead. He may be physically at home only to have his mind at the office. Always trying to solve one problem or another, he is never truly at home. He may also spend all of his off-duty time trying to enhance his skills, and thus his achievement capacity at the office. This was the case with Mark.

When Mark and Kathy came to my office their marriage was in crisis. To use Kathy's words, she was "fed up." She had had enough. Things had to change or else she was going to leave Mark and their marriage of nine years. What was it that had Kathy so upset? Why was she so angry? I'll let her explain:

> Mark has always been an achiever. When I met him in college, he was at the top of his class. In fact, I even admired him for his desire for excellence. Wow, have I ever changed.
>
> I guess things began to sour after the first few years of marriage. Initially, I could understand his need to establish himself in his career at my expense. But after a while, things began to get old.
>
> Then Mark wanted to go to graduate school. He said it would make all the difference in his career and our home life. If he could get an advanced degree, he could "let up"

on the job. The excessive striving could cease. So, with these promises, he went back to school.

Graduate school was a real depressing time. I never saw Mark. He was always in class or studying. But I guess that was to be expected. Of course, he graduated with honors.

The real letdown has come since graduation. He now has the better job . . . more money, more prestige, and *more time away from home*. If anything, things are *worse* than they've ever been . . . not better. Mark works longer hours, is always attending continuing-education conferences, and constantly reads when at home. I've finally realized that things are never going to change. He's driven to be the best. I just wish he felt the same way about his marriage.

Industrious, responsible, hard driving . . . getting to the top requires a great deal . . . sometimes too much. Mark is an example of this. All of these endeavors are examples of success at any cost. Marriages are relegated to exist in the shadows of other aspirations and fail to develop in the manner in which they should, ending up drifting into destruction.

Worthy Causes

Preoccupations with worthy causes can be another way in which we contribute to the hecticness of our lives. Now, I have to tread very gingerly on this topic because, for the Christian, there is no worthier cause than the Church. And if it sounds as if I am denouncing church involvement, I am being totally mis-understood. This is not my intent. As with the previous examples, my concern is with the excessive aspect of otherwise very legitimate endeavors.

Never before in the history of man have there been so many worthy causes and activities. In regard to our children alone there are scouts, T-ball, football, soccer, parent-teacher organizations, room mothers, etc. More service-oriented endeavors include raising money for various medical foundations, assisting with local telephone crisis lines, helping in food-and-clothing distribution centers. The list is extensive and I haven't even mentioned the Church yet. Once the Church is included, the list multiplies. The number of people required to run a church is truly amazing. There are teachers, choir members, board members, ushers, musicians, department leaders, custodians, and so on, all of whom are essential.

There is no question that the activities listed above are worthy and deserving of our involvement. In one way or another, they all contribute to the needs of humanity and the betterment of our society. Furthermore, most of these activities are dependent upon volunteer involvement. If it were not for concerned and committed individuals, worthy causes would disappear. Yet, with the multitude of worthy demands, it is easy for the committed to become **over-committed**. When this occurs, our lives become hectic. When our lives become hectic, our marriages suffer. Somewhere, a line has to be drawn, priorities determined, and costs counted. Failure to do so merely contributes to our hecticness.

The Value System of Our Culture

A final way in which we contribute to our own hecticness is in an acceptance of the crazed value system of our culture. Sometimes our endorsement is in the area of social or status needs. For example, we have to live in better neighborhoods. Our children can go to only the best schools or our entire family wears only the latest fashions. Do not misunderstand me. I am not against any of these things, that is, unless the costs are too high. What is it requiring of our precious time and energy to obtain all of these necessities? How many extra hours are worked to provide these things? Who determines that they are necessities?

Another variation of these status demands is in the activities in which we *must* see our children involved. We place our little girls in ballet, gymnastics, music lessons, and various forms of group activities. We involve our sons in karate, soccer, scouts, and other clubs and organizations. Some of these activities meet throughout the entire year. Others are seasonal. When one ends, we quickly find another "must" to take its place.

Why do we do this? What is it that motivates us as parents to involve our children in multiple activities like the ones just mentioned? Is it not our responsibility as parents to give our children every possible advantage? What would our peers think if our children were not getting just as much enrichment as theirs? What would they think indeed! It seems to me that the real question is not "What would our peers think?" but rather, "How much complexity is this enrichment adding to our lives?"

What does the enrichment cost me in time? What does it cost me in emotional energy? What does it take away from my family? How much more hectic does it make my life? Is it worth it? My sister-in-law found a quote which so impressed her that she hung it on her wall:

> If a mother's place is in the home,
> why am I always in the car?

If we are not careful, enrichment can be too costly . . . at least, emotionally. We are constantly in a battle to determine priorities. Some of our decisions only contribute to our hecticness problem.

Another way in which we demonstrate our acceptance of the crazed value system of our culture is in our endorsement of the belief that a fast-paced life is the norm to be achieved. Do you know anyone who consistently drives the speed limit on the interstate? I don't. We are constantly in a hurry. We live with an expectancy that we are supposed to be busy. Sometimes we almost feel a little embarrassed if our schedules have a few holes in them. "Oops! Nothing scheduled for two o'clock today. Guess I'd better hurry up and get something to fill it in. I've got to be normal. I've got to be busy."

Hecticness is a problem of our age. But, as I have indicated above, oftentimes we contribute to our already hectic life-style. We do it for the family; we do it for ourselves; we do it because we are committed; and we do it because our culture tells us to. We are stressed. We may do it for good and legitimate reasons. But we do it nonetheless. In a very real sense, we do it *to* ourselves.

We are ordinary people with extraordinary demands. Some of these demands are purely circumstantial. There seems to be little that we can do about them. At other times, however . . . and far too often . . . we can only blame ourselves for our problems. And what are the results in regard to our marriages? We drift.

The By-Products of Hecticness

Hecticness produces four major by-products which work together to attack a marriage. The attack is subtle, yet effective. Cooperatively, these by-products foster drifting, and with the emergence of this failing scenario, destruction is not far behind.

Diminished Awareness

One of the by-products produced by a hectic life-style is a diminished awareness of what is happening around us. We tend to lose our consciousness of time. How long has it been since you last sat knee-to-knee and eye-to-eye with your mate and talked about something other than the bills or mundane problems? How long has it been since you really shared something important with one another . . . something meaningful from the depths of your heart?

How long has it been since you really communicated with one another?

My wife has always tended to surpass me in the area of insight. I have often jokingly stated that the two of us should be combined into a single person. With her discernment and my training, we would make a fairly good marriage counselor. It was Jan who first assessed the three years we spent in my doctoral program as being bad for our marriage. As I look back over the experience, I can agree with her assessment. But it took me a little while to figure out *why* this time had been bad.

We were not unaccustomed to hardship. During the six years of marriage preceding my return to full-time graduate work, we had encountered more than our share of crises . . . unexpected career changes, unexpected church disruption, unexpected deaths, and unexpected births. Yet, in all of these crises, we had drawn closer together. The result had been a strengthening as individuals and as a couple. But graduate school was different.

Unlike the crisis experiences, graduate school was the ultimate of hecticness. The pace which accompanied being a full-time student and the primary support of my family was constant and horrid. I was totally engulfed by external demands. For me, those three years are only a blur . . . at least, in regard to my wife and children.

When I entered school, my son was three years of age and my daughter was six months. When I left campus, they were six and three-and-one-half. I do not remember much about them during those three years. When I entered school, Jan and I had been married for six years. When we left campus, we had been married for nine. I do not remember much about our relationship during those three years. Somehow, I lost three years of my life. They escaped me.

It's not difficult to figure out what happened . . . at least, not now. At the time, however, it seemed to be beyond my comprehension. Hecticness diminished my awareness. And as my wife accurately assessed, it was not a good experience for our marriage. Fortunately, it was not as devastating as it could have been. We survived it. Hopefully, we are wiser from the experience. Still, hecticness always takes its toll. Even if there are no scars, I will never regain those three years.

Routine Behavior

A second by-product of hecticness deals with our actions toward one another. Behaviorally, our mate-to-mate interaction takes on a very routine nature. We go through all the motions and we touch all the bases, but there is little meaning or thought behind our enactments. The good-bye kiss, the "Hello, I'm home," the hug at night . . . these are only mechanical observances of an era gone by. We respond to one another out of habit . . . and not emotion.

The absence of emotion and any genuine intent of expression are the underlying themes of routine behavior. These habitual efforts are given little thought. We just do them. Perfunctorily, routinely, automatically . . . we respond to one another with mechanical precision. Hecticness has robbed us of the significance of our behavior. These actions no longer have positive meaning. They merely act as benchmarks of a present situation . . . a relationship suffering from the constancy of external demands.

Sometimes hecticness is so thorough in its demands that even these rote and routine behaviors disappear. The good-bye kiss gets lost in the hurry and scurry of getting the kids to school on time. The "Hello, I'm home" fails to be uttered as your husband exhaustedly seeks out his easy chair. The good-night hug fails to occur as you both collapse into bed. Inch by inch the connectedness dissolves. And with this dissolution, drifting unfolds.

Emotional Numbness

Emotional numbness is another by-product of hecticness. Constant and steady demands take their toll in regard to how we feel toward one another. Step by step, our excessive preoccupation with the externals anesthetizes our emotions. We do not develop negative feelings. Quite the contrary, we have no feelings at all. Gradually, little emotion is either felt or expressed. Our relationship takes on a dry and barren countenance.

This description sounds rather dismal. It should. An emotionless relationship is not what was bargained for when marriage was contemplated. Passion, caring, vibrant and lively feelings . . . these were the characteristics envisioned in the marital relationship. These were the things desired . . . the things expected. This being the case, emotional numbness is definitely a poor substitute.

Loss of Interpersonal Skills

A final by-product of hecticness is the loss of interpersonal skills. I find it interesting that during courtship, future mates are affectionate, attentive, and conversant. Yet, after a few years of marriage, these behaviors have greatly subsided. What were once common and natural become *un*common and *un*natural. Although the changes in how mates relate to one another is precipitated by many variables, the hectic life-style which couples often live has to be considered a primary culprit.

The failure to utilize relational or interpersonal skills often results in what I refer to as *atrophy*. Primarily a medical term, a partial definition would be the following:

1. the decrease in size or wasting away of a body part;
2. the arrested development or loss of a part or organ incidental to the normal development or life of an animal.

Your familiarity with this term is probably more in its physical context. If portions of our body are not routinely exercised we can lose the use of them. A perfectly healthy individual who refuses to walk will soon begin to lose the functioning of his legs. Failure to use an arm will ultimately result in the inability to either lift or hold an object. When this occurs, we say that atrophy has set in.

This concept of atrophy is also applicable to the way in which we relate to one another interpersonally. Not infrequently, I encounter divorced individuals who are attempting to adjust to their newly acquired life-style. Entering the world of the formerly married requires a great many adaptations. One of the more anxious aspects of their adjustment is in reentering the dating market. There are many aspects of this entire reentry area which prompt discomfort, but I am constantly amazed at the number of people who specifically complain that they no longer know how to relate to another individual in an intimate manner, such as:

1. How do you have a meaningful conversation with a man?
2. How do you give your interested attention to a woman?
3. How do you display some degree of affection toward a "significant other"?

These questions come from people who, for the most part, once knew how to do all these things. They are not particularly inept. They are just victims of atrophy. I doubt that much of this form of behavior was taking place in their marriage. It is a case of skills being lost through lack of use. By trying to meet multiple external demands and excessively tending to the cares of this life, we often fail to find the time to relate to one another in an intimate manner. Given enough time, we may forget how to entirely.

What You Can Do

Evaluate Your Situation

As with all other areas of significance, there are no easy solutions for dealing with the problem of hecticness.

The first step in solving any problem is the recognition that you do, in fact, have a problem. You be the judge. Follow the two self-examination steps listed below and assess what is going on in your marriage.

1. Check for the by-products. The by-products of hecticness have been thoroughly elaborated upon in this chapter. Think about the descriptions and then reflect upon your marriage. Are there any similarities? Any comparisons?

Do not let this by-product checkup end with just a self-examination. Discuss your findings with your mate. Together, discuss whether your respective awareness has diminished. How does each of you view the behavioral interaction within the marriage? Is it routine or is it reflective of something far more intentional and meaningful? Has emotional numbness set in? If so, who is the most anesthetized? Have the interpersonal skills decreased? Who is the most negligent? Why?

You be the judge. This is important data. It's important, that is, if you want a healthy marriage.

2. Assess your life-style. Are you busy? Do you feel stressed out? Are you constantly on the go? Is there never enough time to get things done? Even when things do "get done," have you short-changed your mate and children to make these accomplishments? Maybe you are too busy.

What is it that you are investing so much of yourself into? Is it really that important? Is it a career; the accumulation of things; the striving for personal accomplishment? When you count the costs emotionally and relationally, is it worth it?

Remember, our problem is often with the excessive involvement in very legitimate endeavors. As a couple, evaluate your life-style in regard to its hecticness. Ask yourselves the question, "Are we too busy?" Then ask, "What is it that we are so busy doing?"

Finally, ask whether you may be contributing to your problem by endorsing one (or more) of the legitimate attitudes discussed in this chapter:

- doing it for the family
- doing it for personal achievement
- doing it for worthy causes
- doing it because our culture tells us to

Too much attention is given to the cares of this life. This can be disastrous relationally. Remember that as you evaluate your life-style.

Prioritize

One thing the world will not do is to give your marriage a priority position in life. If your relationship is esteemed, it is because you have made it so. If it is prized, it is because you prize it. If you and your mate have had the desperately needed time to interact with one another in a meaningful manner, it is not because our culture decided to give it to you. It is because you took it. Prioritizing is a way of life. In a very real sense, we are always in the process of prioritizing. We are constantly at work determining what is important to us and what is not. And the product of our decision making is evidenced by what, or whom, we invest our time and energies into.

In a practical way, this entire chapter has been devoted to prioritizing as a way of life. Some of our decisions are deliberate and well thought out. Others are not. Some of the consequences of the decisions we make are fully recognized in advance of our decisive actions. Others are not. Regardless of the degree of premeditation, prioritization is achieved—and with the prioritization, the quality of life.

Couples who place their relationship in a high-priority position have the greatest potential for achieving what they want out of the marriage. Those who do not, have a lesser potential. It's as simple as that. High priority offers no guarantees . . . but the odds certainly do get better. Once again, if your marriage is truly valued, it is because *you* have decided to value it. Its priority is recognized by what you give it in time and energy. Your genuine investment will tell the story! Those of you who do not place your marriage in a place of high priority will drift.

— 7 —
DEALING
WITH
ANGER

What is anger?

Is anger natural and normal?

Is it deviant?

What about Christians and anger?

Do Christians get angry?

Is anger sin?

Why do we get angry?

Where does it come from?

Is anger always bad?

Can anger be good?

These are but a few of the many questions which I am frequently asked whenever the subject of anger is discussed with a group of people. Even in a day of increased awareness and understanding, there are still topics which remain confusing. Anger is one of these topics.

What Is Anger?

Anger is defined in the following manner: "a strong feeling of displeasure." Webster's dictionary offers a further statement of clarification indicating that, as the emotional reaction of extreme displeasure, the term in no way suggests either a definite degree of *intensity* or a necessarily outward *manifestation*. Simply stated, anger is an emotion . . . it is not a behavior. Anger is something that we feel. It is not something that we do. Anger comes over us in the same manner as any other emotion. Sadness, joy, happiness . . . all of these feelings, like anger, represent the emotional aspect of our being.

The following diagram illustrates the complexity of the individual. As individuals, we are constantly in the midst of situations or circumstances. In human response to these situations, we (as individuals) think, feel, and behave. As a result of our thinking, feeling, and behaving, there are consequences.

Although there is a great deal of debate concerning which of the three central areas comprising the individual is of the greatest importance (thinking, feeling, or behaving), it is quite accepted that all occur and that each of these areas influences the others. How

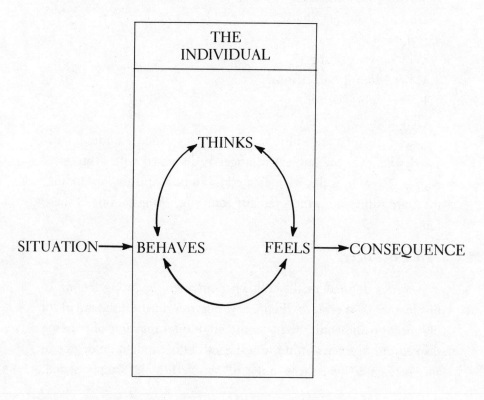

you think affects how you behave and feel. How you feel affects how you think and behave. And how you behave affects how you feel and think. Yet, even though there is a clear interaction among these three areas, each one is still a distinctly separate entity. Behaviors are not thoughts, thoughts are not feelings, and feelings are not behaviors.

With this brief explanation of human behavior, let me reassert what I stated earlier. Anger is an emotion. It is something which is felt.

Is Anger Natural and Normal?

Since anger is an emotion, it is acknowledged as being both natural and normal. Becoming angry does not mark an individual as being deviant any more than becoming happy does. Both are considered natural responses.

To assert that anger is normal and natural, however, should not be perceived as license. There are times when anger does in fact represent deviancy, either in the *individual* or in the *situation*. For example, there are some individuals who tend to become displeased far more easily than others. Whether it be with people or circumstances, their frustration tolerance is quite low. Seemingly trivial matters inappropriately prompt displeasure and anger. A husband who becomes incensed with rage at the mere questioning of a decision is an example of inappropriate anger. Excessiveness in this regard should not be lightly endorsed as "normal."

On the other hand, some individuals who are typically very normal (nonexcessive) in the manner in which they are angered, may find themselves in excessively frustrating situations. For example, a husband who witnesses an unwarranted verbal attack upon his wife may "lose it" emotionally and explode at the attacker. Responding largely to extreme circumstance, the degree of anger he experiences may be abnormal for him. This is definitely a case of excessive situation.

121

As you can see, even within the realm of normality, abnormality can occur. But placing the extremes of individual and situation aside, it should be noted that the normal emotional response to displeasure is anger. Anger is not deviant. It is natural and should be accepted as such.

What About Christians and Anger?

Part of the Christian's confusion regarding anger is the result of an erroneous theological heritage. Within the context of the Church, anger has historically had a negative connotation:

"Christians do not get angry."

"Being angry does not display 'Christlikeness.' "

"Anger is sinful and must be forgiven."

The attitude of anger being evil is illustrated by the old gospel song "Glorious Freedom":

Freedom from pride and all sinful follies;
Freedom from love and glitter of gold;
Freedom from evil temper and anger;
Glorious freedom, rapture untold!

Although only one of the many songs which express the same sentiment, it serves as an example of the way in which many people once thought . . . and some people still think.

Even though the songwriter referred to anger as evil and something from which Jesus brought "glorious freedom," it is fortunate that much of Christendom accepts a less critical view today. There is growing realization that being Christian does not exempt one from normal humanity. Christians, like everyone else, also become angry. Acknowledging Paul's admonition to "be angry and sin not" (Ephesians 4:26), we now recognize that the real danger is not in anger itself (as an emotion), but rather in how it is handled. And with this insight has come further realization that anger, in and of itself, is not sinful.

Why Do We Get Angry?

Let me begin by asking two questions: What is it that makes you angry? When you are angered, what is usually occurring? Take a moment to think about your answers.

Basically, all of your answers can be placed into one of three categories. Your anger is the result of either (1) frustration, (2) hurt, or (3) fear. Anger is never the first thing that you feel. Anger is a secondary emotion. This means that it is always preceded by and, therefore, follows a primary emotion. Becoming frustrated, hurt, or fearful (primary emotions) will frequently lead to feelings of anger.

It is not too difficult to recognize how this applies to marital relationships. Take *frustration*, for instance. Unmet expectations, having to make adjustments, problematic interferences . . . all of these situations can cause frustration and, in turn, lead to anger. Ironically, today's increased expectation of what marriage is supposed to offer has also heightened the likelihood that frustration will occur within the relationship. If little is expected, there is little about which to become frustrated. However, if a great deal is expected, the chances for frustration will increase. This is our present dilemma.

Anger is also the by-product of emotional *hurt*.

"You're a lousy wife."

"You can't do anything right."

"You make me sick."

123

These are statements which cause emotional pain. Being the recipient of personal rejection, thoughtless words, careless deeds . . . any of these incidents can cause a mate to feel deeply hurt. With the pain comes anger.

Over the years, the precipitant of *fear* has changed. Whereas fear used to be activated primarily by circumstances requiring physical self-protection (defense against wild animals or those who wished to do us physical harm), its present-day variation is more concerned with "psychological" self-protection. Fear today is far more likely to occur when threat upon self-esteem is perceived. Today's mates are far more likely to be "put down" by their marital partners than they are to be physically assaulted by them. This does not make the occurrence of a put-down any less feared. Nor does it minimize the anger which ensues. Fear, regardless of the precipitant, will lead to anger.

All three of these common occurrences—frustration, hurt, and fear—prompt angered emotions. We do not like the precipitants. And our dislike causes us to become angry. Natural . . . normal . . . predictable . . . it comes from deep within us. It is the way we were created to be. And it is how we are.

Is Anger Bad?

There are times when anger is bad. The inappropriate responses of immature individuals or the unusually heightened emotion experienced by a person subjected to an extreme situation causing him to "lose it" are both well deserving of the negative connotation of anger. However, these are examples of excesses. There are few things which, regardless of how good they may be in moderation, would not also be found to be deviant in nature when pushed to an extreme form.

I have often wondered whether it would be possible to do away with anger altogether. Could a person be so in control of his/her life as to never become frustrated, hurt, or fearful? I have come to the conclusion that this is not only improbable but also undesirable. To attempt to channel anger, to try to become angry in moderation, to work toward appropriate resolution of angry feelings . . . these are desirable goals. But to eliminate anger altogether . . . never.

Anger serves a very useful purpose. It functions as a motivator. Through personal discomfort, anger first informs us that there are things which we do not like . . . things which may need correcting. It then gives us the impetus to deal with them. Through anger, we are energized to act. It implores us to make things better, whether the "better" be with relationships or situations. At least, this is its positive and healthy potential. Granted, we do not need anger in its excessiveness. But we do need anger.

If I were to make a statement which would summarize all that I have said regarding anger thus far and also prepare the way for all that remains to be said, it would be this: Anger is normal . . . resolving it is not so normal.

How We Respond When Angry

- Do not know what to do.
- Do not want to do anything different.
- Deny that we are angry.
- Know what to do but just can't seem to do it.
- Do not see a need to do things any differently.
- Mistakenly believe that what is being done is the best or right way to respond.

It is not always easy to answer the question of why people mishandle their anger. Some of the more common reasons are listed above. By designating what people do, we are able to identify that behavior which is both helpful and appropriate . . . and that behavior which is not helpful and, therefore, inappropriate. When it comes to dealing with our anger, there are some things which should definitely be done . . . and there are other things which definitely should not.

Whenever I approach the task of suggesting how we should deal with our anger, I rely heavily on assertiveness philosophy. Although assertiveness extends far beyond the limited scope of merely dealing with anger, I believe it provides a stable foundation upon which to base our attempt at handling this troublesome issue.

The assertiveness philosophy and assertiveness training began to make its appearance in the 1960s. Since its inception, there have been a number of misconceptions concerning exactly what it purports to accomplish. Some have seen it only as a part of the women's liberation movement. Others have viewed it as fostering selfishness with total disregard for the rights and feelings of others. In reality, neither of these perceptions is accurate.

First, the scope of the assertiveness philosophy includes all persons who desire to (1) improve their effectiveness in getting along with others, (2) improve how they feel about themselves, and (3) increase the probability of getting what they want. Second, standing up for one's rights is not, in itself, selfish. It could be selfish if it were done with no concern for the needs and rights of others, but a genuinely assertive person will be concerned about the rights and feelings of those with whom he is interacting. He is careful not to take a stand just for the sake of taking a stand, but attempts to do what he believes to be the best thing for the relationship. Therefore, a person who is attempting to live assertively attempts to behave in a manner that will not only enable him to feel good about himself but also will offer the best opportunity for the enhancement of the entire relationship.

Man is fully capable of misusing and abusing anything regardless of its potential for good. Those within the Church should be keenly aware of this fact. I shudder to think of the many atrocities which have been committed in the exploited name of Christianity. Assertiveness is not exempt from such exploitation. Many misdeeds have been justified under the guise of assertive behavior. Yet its intent, as well as its precepts, are sound.

Basically, assertive philosophy states that (1) people have rights and (2) they ought to claim them:

- the right to be treated with respect
- the right to make mistakes
- the right to have and express feelings
- the right to say no
- the right to ask why
- the right to have and express opinions

These are but a few of the rights to which we are entitled, yet are frequently denied. Sometimes these rights are denied us by those around us. At other times, we are guilty of denying them to ourselves. Entitlement does not ensure possession. A right is not ours until we claim it. And the theme of assertiveness is that we ought to claim our rights.

The assertiveness philosophy emphasizes the importance of appropriate communication between people. It suggests that if people can learn better ways of communicating their likes, dislikes, thoughts, feelings, and desires, they can then improve their relationships with others. This concept is what makes assertiveness so applicable to our problem of dealing with anger. As I have repeatedly stated, our problem is not with the existence of anger as an emotion, but with what we *do* with our anger. Assertiveness emphasizes the doing. In short, it claims that there is a best way to behave or act when you are angry.

From an assertiveness perspective, all of our actions or behaviors can be grouped into one of three categories. We are either behaving aggressively, nonassertively, or assertively. As we better understand the nature of each of these behaviors, we will clearly recognize what is best for us to do.

Aggressive Behavior

Aggressive behavior is any action which violates the rights of others. It is this form of behavior which we usually mistakenly think of whenever we imagine people getting angry. Those who behave aggressively when angry often say harsh things. They are belligerent and intimidating. They "blow others away." I wonder if this isn't, at least in part, what Peter was referring to in his first epistle:

> If you suffer, it must not be for murder, theft, or sorcery, nor for infringing the rights of others.
>
> 1 Peter 4:15

Aggressive behavior fits within the context of this Scripture. It definitely infringes on the rights of others. However, it is interesting to note that not all aggressive behavior is as direct as that mentioned above. Some prefer a more indirect expression. Those who express their anger in an indirectly aggressive manner do so by dragging their feet, by displaying interfering and sabotaging maneuvers, and by saying sweet things with negative underlying and implied meanings. "I think you look very attractive [pause] for someone who is a little overweight." Although not so obvious as its more direct counterpart, this form of aggression is equally nonproductive.

With some of us, aggressive behavior is intentional and aimed at either getting what we want or avoiding an issue through domination. We use it. With others of us, however, it seems to be more of a spontaneous and uncontrollable response. We just react. But regardless of the "whys," it is damaging.

Aggressiveness always gets us in trouble. We may get what we want, but it is at a high cost. The wife may give in or the husband may feel better after getting it off his chest. But the "I win—you lose" arrangement, which is predicated on aggressively dealing with anger, always damages the marital relationship. For some reason, we simply do not like to be intimidated. And a damaged relationship is a high price to pay for any perceived gain.

Nonassertive Behavior

Nonassertive behavior presents a sharp contrast to the aggressive actions just described. As opposed to violating the rights of others, nonassertive behavior involves the giving up of personal rights. Although anger is a natural and healthy human emotion, those who deal nonassertively with their anger are in a very real sense denying themselves this right. Mates who deal nonassertively with their anger usually do so with the aid of a number of justifications. Unfortunately, regardless of the rationale, this behavior, much like aggressiveness, is nonproductive for the relationship.

The goal of nonassertive behavior is usually to please people or to avoid conflict. Sometimes we accomplish this goal by sitting on our anger. We know that we are angry and we know what has angered us. But we choose not to deal directly with our problem. One of the most common justifications for this behavior is the belief that to behave in any other manner would not be the nice thing to do. Nonassertive people are often obsessed with doing the nice thing. My experience has been that there are some mates who are quite simply too nice for their own good, as well as for the best interest of the relationship.

Another rationale for not dealing with anger is that it won't do any good anyway. In essence, an angry husband rationalizes away any intent of dealing honestly with his wife. "It won't change anything. She'll just keep on doing what she's always done. Why should I go through the hassle of talking to her about it?" Believing that to behave in any other fashion would not improve his situation, he feels very justified in avoiding it all together.

Another way in which we often see nonassertive behavior is through the use of denial. This is where we refuse to admit to being angry at all. "What? Me angry? Are you kidding? Of course I'm not angry." If we deny that we are angry, then we do not have to deal with it. We must remember that for some Christians, anger is still seen as sinful. And rather than be caught in sin, they will simply deny the presence of an otherwise normal and natural response to frustration, hurt, and fear.

One of the things which seems to prolong the nonassertive

handling of our anger is the thought that behaving in this manner will keep us out of trouble. Nothing could be further from the truth. Anger is like burning a fire in the fireplace of your home. The burning logs represent the intensity of your angry feelings at the time you are angered. Much like the logs, your anger burns brightly for a while. There is heat . . . there is brilliance . . . there is energy. But given an ample amount of time, the flames subside and the fire wanes. Finally, the fire goes out.

We inaccurately imagine that our anger follows a similar course. If we only sit on our anger, we will cool off and it will go away. We believe that by behaving nonassertively with our anger, we will avoid conflict and trouble in our relationship. Unfortunately, this is not the case. Much like the fire, your anger will subside. You will become cordial or even cooperative. It will appear as though nothing ever happened . . . it is business as usual. Everything is fine. Unfortunately, the anger is still there.

To handle anger in this manner is only to mishandle it. Anger which is avoided or denied never totally disappears. Unresolved anger always leaves a residue. Wood fires never burn clean. Just as burning logs will always leave ashes, unresolved anger will also leave a reminder. Failing to clean out the fireplace will have its consequences. Can you see why I say dealing with your anger nonassertively is counterproductive? One remembrance, when added to the numerous other remembrances from similar episodes of sitting on it, will slowly burn a relationship.

Assertive Behavior

Assertive behavior involves standing up for your rights. This theme presents difficulty for some Christians. It is a strong statement and if pushed to an extreme, it becomes even stronger. We push it to an extreme by implying that you *always have to (must)* stand up for your rights. This is simply not the case.

The entire assertiveness philosophy is based on "rights." Everyone has them. You have the right to do this or that and also to be allowed to do this or that. If this is true, then you obviously also have the right to choose *not to claim your rights*. How can this be done in an assertiveness framework? Quite simply, the pivotal issue in assertion is that of *choice*. Who is it who makes your decisions? Is it you who makes them or are they being made for you? Jesus, who lived and died according to an assertive life-style, gives us a clear example of this. He expounds on this theme of choice when referring to His role as the good shepherd:

> The Father loves me because I lay down my life, to receive it back again. No one has robbed me of it; I am laying it down of my own free will. I have the right to lay it down, and I have the right to receive it back again; this charge I have received from my Father.
>
> John 10:17, 18

Jesus was not forced to die. He chose to. He willingly gave up His life and His right to live for the best interest of mankind. Being the Son of God, He had the power to stop His execution. But He chose not to.

Sometimes you may feel that giving up your rights in a particular situation is the best thing to do. And maybe it is. This is a choice which is your right to make. However, you need to be sure that it is the best choice . . . that it is a choice that **you** are making as opposed to one being made **for** you . . . and that it is a choice based on sound justification as opposed to merely finding an excuse for avoiding a difficult situation. Choosing to relinquish a right can fit into an assertive life-style, but it can easily become a point of rationalization as well.

When standing up for your rights, you say what you think, how you feel, and what you believe in ways that are direct, honest, and appropriate. And you *do* what you think you should do. Others' rights are not violated. Respect is shown for your own rights as well as the rights of others. The goals of acting assertively are to feel better about yourself, to maintain or improve good relationships with others, and to increase the possibility of getting what you really want.

Attempting to behave assertively, a husband who is angered by the actions of his wife will deal directly with the problem. Whereas an aggressive husband might verbally "blow his wife away" and a nonassertive husband might deny that anger even exists, an assertive mate will confront the marital partner.

Peter and Susan provide us an illustration of assertion:

> Susan, I am pretty frustrated and I think we need to talk about it. You said you wanted me home by five o'clock so we could leave the house in time for our dinner reservations. I changed my appointments at work to be able to do that. Yet, you didn't get here until six o'clock because you were busy shopping. Now we're going to be late. I find this situation very frustrating. Can you help me with this?

In love, Peter honestly confronted his wife. He could have chosen to behave differently. Instead of confronting her in this manner, he could have aggressively blown her away. "I don't know why I ever married you. You're so irresponsible. . . ." This undoubtedly would have made for a poor rest of the evening. On the other hand, Peter could have chosen to nonassertively avoid the situation. He could have acted as if nothing had happened. Had he done this, however, his anger would have continued to eat away at him. When it comes to relationships, tension and closeness are contradictory terms. Choosing to deal with Susan as he did had far more potential for good than either of the other two choices.

Aggressive, nonassertive, assertive . . . anytime you become angry with your mate, you deal with your anger in one of these three ways. You either attack, avoid, or "speak the truth in love." The last of these is the most productive. Dealing with a mate honestly, directly, and appropriately clearly offers the greatest opportunity for growth in a marriage. Failing to behave in this assertive manner will always produce negative, possibly disastrous consequences.

Failing to Resolve Anger: The Consequences

Anger is potentially a very positive and useful force. The bright side of anger is displayed when it (1) *acts as a signal* and alerts us to the fact that something is not right, and (2) *energizes* us to act. As a result of anger, we try to make our personal world better.

Anger also has a dark side . . . a potential for harm and destruction. One of the ways in which anger shows its dark side is through mishandling, as shown in the preceding section. You will remember my claim that angry feelings are always dealt with . . . they are handled aggressively, nonassertively, or assertively. The aggressive and nonassertive forms of handling are actually examples of mishandling. They are counterproductive. They destroy rather than build. They are the dark side of anger.

Another form of the dark side of anger is the *failure to resolve anger*. Although more subtle a foe than its mishandling counterpart, its potential for damage within relationships is much more far-reaching. It is a true adversary to a healthy marriage.

By *resolve*, I am referring to the dispelling or clearing up of the angry feelings themselves. When handled appropriately, angry feelings tend to dissolve . . . they subside and go away. Granted, sometimes this requires a little time. Yet, even in extreme cases, the process of healing is progressive. Improvement can be noted. Anger serves its purpose and, once its task is completed, it disappears. This is the natural course of action.

Regardless of the form of mishandling which allows anger to move from something positive to something negative, the consequences are just as staggering. I believe the following to be the four most potent reasons we must resolve our anger.

Interferes With Perception of Our Mate

One consequence of unresolved anger is the emergence of perceptual distortion. By this I mean that the view which we have of our mate becomes distorted. Metaphorically, this phenomenon is similar to an unfortunate experience I once had. I had taken some pictures while at a retreat. After my film was processed, I found one of the snapshots to be terribly out of focus. Everything on the photo was blurred. There were brown blobs instead of mountains; broccoli-appearing forms which were supposed to be trees; and four spheres which were probably faces. What was intended to be a memorable masterpiece of photographic art ended instead as an out-of-focus mess. Everything in my picture was blurred. Everything, that is, except for one item. Somehow, amidst the photographic chaos, a bird managed to emerge unscathed. In the middle of fuzzy mountains, trees, and faces, a darting passerby (definitely an uninvited guest) became the center of attention.

The bird was picture perfect. The clarity of his features poignantly attested to the fact that the camera was in fact *not* out of focus. Unfortunately, however, the focus of the camera was narrowly directed at the object which was closest to the lens and not at those whom I had intended. The panoramic view of mountains and trees had been breathtaking. Yet, this fact could not be proved by the photo which I had taken. Although the faces of my friends had been covered with exuberant expressions, the camera failed to take note. All that seemed to matter to my camera was the object which flew before it. The finished product, therefore, was a distinctively clear picture of a bird.

It is not unusual for this same kind of perceptual distortion to occur when we become angry with our mate. "You're *always* insensitive!" "You *never* cooperate with me!" "I can't *ever* trust you!" Actually, none of these mates are really "always," "never," or "ever" anything. It is simply a case of distorted perception. In the heat of the moment, the irritating mate is seen from this extreme position.

When I become angry with Jan, I often fail to see things as they truly are. My reality becomes distorted. Her admirable qualities . . . her compassionate acts . . . her giving and cooperative attitude . . . all of the things about her which are good seem to disappear from my sight. Instead of recognizing what is in fact a more accurate reality, I can only focus on what she has done to anger me so. At times like these, my vision is definitely blurred.

Interestingly, it makes little difference whether my anger is well founded or not. Whether rational or irrational; legitimate or illegitimate; warranted or unwarranted, my reaction is still the same. I am upset. I am intense. And I am uncomfortable. Similar to the camera illustration, my focus is narrowly directed at the point of my anger and until the anger is resolved, there will be a block in our relationship.

Anger is a powerful emotion. It must be resolved. Failing to do so can result in permanent visual damage. And perceptual distortion is destructive to a relationship. For marriage to flourish and to avoid the potential to drift, mates must see one another with clarity.

Fosters Development of Resentment

Another consequence of failing to resolve anger is the development of resentment. Anger and resentment are sometimes confused with one another. This is a grave error. Resentment is a malignancy which must be eradicated as opposed to being a healthy emotion which can run a productive course if allowed.

Anger is situation specific. It is precipitated by a single incident. It is a healthy response to a hurt, a fear, or a frustration. Resentment, on the other hand, is more general. It needs no current precipitant, for it is always present. Over time, the accumulation of many instances of unresolved anger has produced a seething hostility which watches and waits for an opportunity to express itself. Like a cancer which slowly consumes the body, it is omnipresent.

Dan and Kay had spoken with me informally on several occasions before finally setting an official counseling appointment. Dan really did not see the need for talking with a professional but if that was what Kay wanted to do, he was willing to participate.

In our previous informal contacts, Dan and Kay had been pleasant toward each other and with me. In the session attitudes began to change and Dan remained pleasant enough but Kay became very intense. She sat on the side of her chair and leaned away from Dan. She almost had her back turned toward him. It was as though her physical posture demonstrated her emotional stance in the marriage.

Kay began by listing—extensively—all of the things which she disliked about Dan. Dan sat in his chair in near shock. When Kay began to wind down, Dan asked her if there was anything that she *didn't* dislike about him. Kay didn't respond. The room then grew very silent. Kay was obviously angry with Dan but I had not seen anything that even closely resembled a precipitant significant enough to warrant such intensity. If that were the case, then what was she *really* angry about? I suspected that what we were really dealing with was an underlying resentment. Rather than being any *one* thing which bothered Kay, we were actually dealing with a long list of unresolved hurts and frustrations which, over time, had constructed a well-fortified resentment. As it turned out, I was correct. Once we began to get into the history of their relationship, the pieces began to fall together.

There was the geographical relocation that never got resolved. There was Kay's giving up a career that never got resolved. There was the change in financial status that never got resolved. There was Dan's refusal to have surgery which would increase the possibility that he and Kay could have children that never got resolved. As these unresolved incidents accumulated, a seething resentment was born. And from an attitude of resentment, there probably wasn't anything that Dan could do that Kay wouldn't find fault with. She was in a perpetual state of anger.

Dan and Kay's situation ought to help us differentiate between anger and resentment. Anger occurs in an instant whereas resentment requires time to develop. Anger is a reponse to a single precipitant whereas resentment is amassed from many. Anger diminishes in a short period of time whereas resentment is a constant companion. Anger is productive whereas resentment is not. Can you see the difference? As the case of Dan and Kay illustrates, resentment is a product of unresolved anger. If allowed to exist within a marriage, it can bring the relationship to ruin.

The biblical admonition found in Ephesians 4:27 has its best application to this issue of resentment:

> Do not let sunset find you still nursing it [anger]; leave no loophole for the devil.

I cannot say for certain whether Paul's use of the term *sunset* was meant literally or figuratively but I believe that it was the latter.

I believe that there are times when attempting to deal with anger prior to the setting of the sun may be inappropriate and not in the best interest of the mates. Sometimes the lateness of the hour or the tiredness of the day may suggest that the difficulty would best be handled at a later time when freshness of mind could be a welcome asset. And then there are also times when emotions are so heated that a legitimate period of cooling off is warranted so as to facilitate a more cooperative and forgiving spirit of reconciliation. Yet, be this as it may, there is no mistaking of Paul's *intent*. His statement is strong. Presumptuously, I would paraphrase it in this manner:

Do not give your anger a chance to fester. Do not nurse it.
Do not allow it to turn into resentment. Deal with it. And
do so quickly.

Paul knew the destructive power inherent in resentment. But he
also understood the elements involved in its creation and gave a
simple prescription . . . resolve your anger and do so quickly.

Affects More Than the Marriage

Failing to resolve anger can affect more than just the marriage. It
can also affect all of those other people with whom we have contact.
In a rather humorous manner, Bob Benson poignantly illustrates
this fact in his book *Come Share the Being:*

> I read about a man who said he never fussed at an employee
> in the afternoon because he liked dogs. He went on to
> explain that usually what happened was the man went
> home frustrated and fuming and the first thing he did was to
> give his wife a few short answers and this made her mad
> also. About that time the oldest son innocently strolls
> through the kitchen and mom gives him a verbal blast. He
> then seeks out his sister and passes it on. In a little while the
> baby brother comes wandering in and the sister tells him in
> no uncertain terms to let her things alone and stay out of the
> room. And the poor little brother, being the low man on the
> totem pole, starts out into the yard and the dog is asleep on
> the back step so he just kicks the dog. So the employer
> didn't bawl people out in the afternoon because he liked
> dogs.

I am not as concerned about the domino effect illustrated in this
passage as I am with the pervasive influence which anger seems to
have upon the disposition of the one who is angered. It is difficult

to be dry when you are wet. It is difficult to see light where there is darkness. And it is equally difficult to be pleasant and loving when you are angry. Unfortunately for those around us, the anger which we feel usually gets directed at more than just the one who has precipitated it.

Within families, the most noticeable recipients of this displaced anger are the children. Isn't it amazing that it is the ones whom we love the most who are the most vulnerable to our misdirected anger?

Boy, Daddy sure is in a grumpy mood. He jumped all over me for no reason at all.

All I did was leave my backpack in the living room and Mom grounded me for a month. You would have thought I broke a lamp or something.

Overreactions to minor incidents . . . mountains out of mole-hills . . . criticism from out of the blue . . . these are the expressions of displaced anger. This is how we vent in a misdirected fashion. And who gets hurt by this unnecessary and unwarranted behavior? The child . . . and the family. This is a heavy price to pay for simply failing to resolve anger.

Prevents Closeness and Growth

I had been seeing Tom and Jean for a number of months. They had made significant enough progress so as to allow an increasing amount of time between visits. This fact, coupled with holidays and unexpected illnesses, had resulted in two months passing since their last visit. Both of them seemed pleasant enough when we began the session, although Tom was a little quieter than usual. When I asked how things had gone since our last meeting, he was quick to respond. The interchange which ensued went something like this:

> Tom: "I think things have gone pretty good. We haven't been arguing. [Pause] Yet, I've been feeling kind of distant during the past couple weeks."
>
> Therapist: "Distant?"
>
> Tom: "Well, you know. Not real close."
>
> Therapist: "Have you felt the same way, Jean?"
>
> Jean: "I guess I have, a little."
>
> Therapist: "Why do you think you have been feeling distant?"
>
> Tom: "I'm not sure. Maybe I've been too busy with work. Yes, I guess that's the reason."
>
> Therapist: "What do you think, Jean?"
>
> Jean: "Oh, I don't really know."

The entire session had been tentative. Tom and Jean had been cordial enough to one another, but the distance which was alluded to by Tom seemed to be noticeably present in their interaction. Although preoccupation with work may have unpremeditatedly taken its toll, I suspected a far different culprit.

> Therapist: "Well, you know work pressures can definitely impact on a marriage. We've seen how that has been a difficulty for the two of you in the past. It may be that it has reasserted itself once again. However, there may be something else going on. Sometimes an incident may occur between mates which fails to get resolved. When this happens, they tend to feel estranged or distant from one another. Is there something which has occurred that the two of you have failed to deal with?"

The silence which followed my discourse was all that was needed to confirm that I was on the right track. After a strategic pause, I pressed my point to conclusion:

Therapist:	"Well, Tom, can you think of anything?"
Tom:	[No response. He made only a "hmmm" sound.]
Therapist:	"Tom seems to need some help, Jean. Can you think of anything?"
Jean:	"Yes, I can. It happened about six weeks ago." [To Tom:] "Do you remember?"
Tom:	"Yes . . . I do."

What was important for Tom and Jean was not the issue which created their conflict. Rather, it was the fact that they would let the anger which was produced by the conflict persist for six weeks without seeking a satisfactory resolution. For six weeks, there was stress in the marriage. For six weeks, emotional distance was the order of the day. For six weeks, there was cordiality and common courtesy . . . but little more. For six weeks, they preferred to live with emotional tension rather than to deal with a problematic situation. And it was this preference which most alarmed me. For in reality, this preference is far more dangerous to the health of a relationship than is any issue which may emerge.

I do not wish to imply that the issues which prompt conflicts are unimportant. Some are very important. But of greater significance is the anger which is produced by the conflict. The issue which prompted tension between Tom and Jean was important. But the fact that their anger was not resolved was even *more* important.

Not every issue will be resolved. Not every disagreement has a point of common ground. Yet, the anger which ensues must find a resolution. If not, it will lodge itself between mates and rob them of the closeness which they both desire. Closeness and tension are contradictory terms. They cannot coexist.

The final consequence of failing to resolve anger is the prevention of closeness and growth. Like the others, it too can be destructive to a marriage.

Final Thoughts

I have a motto which dictates much of how I relate to my wife:

If it's important enough to get angry about,
it's important enough to deal with.

I have found it to be an effective guideline for our marriage. Distorted perceptions, seething resentment, displaced hostility, emotional distance . . . the consequences of failing to resolve anger are numerous. Any one of these is a villain. Any one attacks the stability of a marriage. And any one is potentially lethal. My goal is to prevent them from occurring.

Some of my comments may have appeared to be idealistic. While acknowledging that not every issue will necessarily be resolved, I implied that the anger which is prompted by the conflict can be. In reality, this too may not always occur. There may be instances where, regardless of the efforts made to resolve the emotional difficulty in the marriage, they will be responded to antagonistically. When noncooperation rules the day, anger will neither easily nor readily disappear. A continued display of insensitivity of this nature will only hasten the emotional demise of a relationship.

Still, things do not have to take this course of action. You do not have to live lives encumbered by unresolved feelings of anger. Most of what transpires between mates in the form of conflict is resolvable. It requires only the willingness to do what needs to be done. With a recognition of the consequences, should there be any hesitancy?

What You Can Do

Deal With Your Anger

Throughout this chapter I have stressed the theme of "deal with your anger." Hand in hand with this theme has been the suggestion that the best way to do this is to be direct and honest. Although many authors have written entire books on the "how to's" of accomplishing this task, David Mace offers a simple three-step procedure which, if used as a model, is fairly applicable to most of our marriages. What follows is a variation of Mace's steps, which he explained in an article called "Marital Intimacy and the Deadly Love-Anger Cycle," *Journal of Marriage and Family Counseling*.

Step 1   Admit the anger.   The first thing which you have to do is to admit to yourself that you are angry. Calling it something other than anger, denying that it exists, rationalizing it away . . . all of these tendencies must be rejected. Until the existence of your anger is acknowledged, you will only "spin your wheels." Your anger must be "owned" before you can move toward resolution.

This issue of ownership is a difficult obstacle for some people. There are many personal, historical, and cultural factors which contribute to a resistance to admitting to what is real. Yet, it is an essential first step. Without the acceptance of ownership, there can be no further progress made toward resolving that which impedes the growth of the relationship.

Step 2   Ask for help.   You are angry. But you do not want to be. You care very deeply for your mate and you want the closeness and comfort that once was present in your relationship to be restored. Therefore, because (1) you value the relationship, (2) your mate is the recipient of your anger, and (3) you do not wish to be angry, you must ask for his/her help in resolving the difficulty.

A simple "I statement" seems to offer the best means of soliciting the help you desire from your mate:

"I am angry but I don't want to be. Will you help me?"

You may choose some variation of this direct approach. But regardless of what you say, it is important that a theme of valuing the relationship above whatever it was which prompted the disagreement be conveyed.

Step 3 Deal with the issue.   Obviously, something has occurred to make you angry. A hurt, a fear, a frustration . . . something has angered you. It is imperative that this be dealt with.

Sometimes the precipitant is clear. A harsh word, a blatantly insensitive act, an unintentional snubbing . . . these are the precipitants which are easily recognized. At other times, however, our ability to identify causes is far more impaired. We are uncertain as to exactly why we are angry . . . we just know that we are. Regardless of the clarity, the issue must be dealt with. Usually, the variables related to the conflict have a way of clarifying themselves once an earnest dealing with the issue is begun.

It is important during these times of confrontation for both of you to stay on task. Old wounds, stored-up hostilities, insignificant red herrings . . . there is no place for these distractions when the business of resolution is under way. Tendencies in these directions must be avoided. Of primary importance are the issue at hand and the pain it has caused. Even if the issue itself is not totally resolved, each of you should have the following goals:

- to express a cooperative attitude toward one another,
- to strive for agreement in regard to whatever prompted the conflict,
- if the issue cannot be settled at that time, to accept disagreement without maintaining hostility, and
- to express an assured commitment to the value of the relationship.

This last point goes a long way toward allowing you to disagree agreeably.

Determine Your Marital Response Style

The following questionnaire has been developed in order to aid you in the assessment of the presence and the handling of anger in your marriage. Both of you are to complete the twelve items which comprise this exercise. There should be no sharing of answers during this phase. After answering all of the items, the question-naires should be exchanged. After a period of examination, the responses should be discussed. Themes for discussion would be as follows:

- How much agreement is there in your answers?
- Where is there disagreement?
- What conclusions can be drawn?
- What changes, if any, need to be made in the way anger is handled?

A discussion of this kind may not be easy. Anger is a difficult topic to deal with. However, the benefits from completing such an exercise can be quite positive. Becoming aware of your marital response style is a first step toward constructive change if in fact change is needed at all.

Marital Response Style

1. Which of the following does my mate most *frequently* do to anger me? (Choose *one* answer.)

    1. Hurts me.
    2. Frustrates me.
    3. Creates fear in me.

2. How frequently does this occur? (Choose *one* answer.)

    1. Seldom.
    2. Occasionally.
    3. Often.
    4. Very often.

3. How do I most *frequently* anger my mate? (Choose *one* answer.)

    1. Hurt him/her.
    2. Frustrate him/her.
    3. Create fear in him/her.

4. How frequently does this occur? (Choose *one* answer.)

    1. Seldom.
    2. Occasionally.
    3. Often.
    4. Very often.

5. How do I know when I am angry? (Write in answer.)

_____

_____

_____

6. How do I know when my mate is angry? (Write in answer.)

_____

_____

_____

7. When angry with my mate, how do I typically respond? (Choose *one* answer.)

    1. I "blow up."
    2. I "sit on it."
    3. I deal honestly and directly with my mate.

8. How does my mate respond to this type of behavior? (Choose *one* answer.)

    1. "Blows up" at me.
    2. "Sits on it."
    3. Deals honestly and directly with me.

9. When my mate is angry with me, what does he/she typically do? (Choose *one* answer.)

    1. "Blows up" at me.
    2. "Sits on it."
    3. Deals honestly and directly with me.

10. How do I usually respond to this type of behavior? (Choose *one* answer.)

    1. I "blow up."
    2. I "sit on it."
    3. I deal with it honestly and directly.

11. What could *I* do to improve how *we* deal with anger in our relationship? (Write in answer.)

_____

_____

_____

12. What could my *mate* do to improve how *we* deal with anger in our relationship? (Write in answer.)

_____

_____

_____

— 8 —
PUSHED
TO
EXTREMES

Clerice and Paul identified "marital conflict" as the reason for seeking counseling on their general information form. There was little evidence of this as we began the first session. As long as the conversation remained superficial, everything appeared cordial enough. However, as the session progressed, the cool and calm composure being projected by the couple quickly gave way to one underscored with anger. Accusations, retorts, barbs . . . their "in session" behavior became increasingly different from that which was presented at the outset.

For all practical purposes, the conflictual behavior was something the couple kept to themselves. When at church or with friends, they were very adept at donning a "things couldn't be better" mask. But at home, behind closed doors, the public facade of an ideal marriage quickly gave way to the reality of disappointment and conflict.

In attempting to explain to me just how the marriage had arrived at its present condition, Clerice and Paul presented the problem from two entirely different vantage points. "He is always preoccupied with his personal interests and never shares himself with me." "She is constantly making demands upon me and, regardless of what I do, it is never enough." From Clerice's point of view, Paul had never given enough to the relationship. From Paul's, Clerice had always wanted too much.

Few couples enter marriage with exactly the same set of expectations. There are always differences. Much of what eventually becomes of the relationship—whether it is satisfying or frustrating, rewarding or confining—is determined by the couple's ability to resolve or reduce these differences. This being the case, some couples seem to find it more difficult to make the needed adjustments than do others.

For Clerice and Paul, ten years of marriage had only broadened the differences between them. Ten years of failing to make necessary adjustments finally prompted them to seek counseling. So there they sat. Both were angry, resentful, and thoroughly frustrated. Accusations flowed with little restraint. Clerice complained, "He's a 'taker' and I'm tired of it," to which Paul responded, "She's constantly on my back and I've had it." Pushed to extremes, the battle lines had been drawn.

Another couple with whom I counseled, Sharon and John, left little doubt that they were in the midst of a marital crisis. Unlike the image presented by Clerice and Paul, there was no appearance of calm or congeniality. When we met for the first session, it was obvious that Sharon had been crying prior to their arrival at my office. The opening attempts at conversation merely provided Sharon the opportunity to continue her weeping. In addition to the identification of marital problems on the general information form, John had added that Sharon was mildly depressed. In the session, John explained that Sharon had better days and worse days, but that most recently the severity of her depression had increased.

John sat rather sheepishly in the room. He seemed to care about Sharon and her apparent emotional difficulties, but it was obvious that the intensity of her feelings was discomforting for him. He did not know what to do or what to say. He felt helpless.

Diverging from the intensity of the moment, I asked each of them to tell me what had led up to the crisis. John was hesitant to say anything. He feared that he might escalate Sharon's already tense condition. Regaining some composure, Sharon proceeded to recount what she perceived to have precipitated their problem. More specifically, she began to enumerate upon John's indiscretions.

From Sharon's report, John was emotionally involved with another woman. This particular "other woman" worked with him. Sharon had first become aware of the involvement a year earlier. She had known that they were friends before that time, but it was only then that she began to suspect that there was more than just a friendship. They worked together, ate lunch together, went to conferences and meetings together, and even played tennis on a regular basis together. In essence, from Sharon's viewpoint, they were always together . . . and that's the way John liked it:

> Anytime I tried to talk with him about my concerns he just laughed. He said I had nothing to worry about, that they were just good friends. When I would get mad and complain, John would say I was overreacting.

A week earlier, in the midst of hysterics, Sharon announced that she and the children were leaving John. It was then that he began to listen.

John's version of what had occurred confirmed the events as described by Sharon but contradicted the suggestion that anything more than a friendship had developed between himself and the other woman:

> We have a lot in common. We have the same career goals and share many of the same opinions on lots of issues. We both even like to play tennis. I asked Sharon to play tennis with me but she said she wasn't interested. So I turned to someone else for a tennis partner. Our relationship is totally

151

innocent but Sharon and I cannot even discuss it without her getting upset. I have done nothing wrong and my relationship at work is totally on a friendship basis. If Sharon were not overreacting as she is, there would be no problem. But if I have to give up my friendship to keep my marriage, I'm willing to do it.

I had the suspicion that the degree to which John was willing to give up the friendship at work was proportionately related to the degree of emotional intensity displayed by Sharon. Being depressed as she was, John would give up his other friendship. He would do anything to keep his marriage intact. If Sharon were calmer, however, John would be less willing to change. In essence, he was not truly willing to give it up at all. He saw the relationship as legitimate and Sharon's request as demanding. But he had no choice. He would rather appease her at this time than suffer the consequences of her wrath.

Inquiring further into their marital history, it was not difficult to make some fairly accurate assumptions about their relationship. Basically, the majority of their eighteen years together had been spent *drifting*. John was wrapped up with his career and Sharon was kept busy with four children. John admitted that he had wanted more out of the relationship. But it seemed that every time he approached Sharon about going out for an evening or getting away for a weekend, she would come up with some reason they could not do it. Not being a persistent individual, he would let the suggestion drop.

Sharon defended herself, citing the difficulties in getting dependable baby-sitters and the financial infeasibility of going somewhere for an entire weekend. "I wasn't against doing things with John. It just wasn't always practical." So they drifted. Neither had been really pleased with the marital relationship, but both had thought it was okay. At least, it was okay until this crisis rocked their marital boat.

I have just described two totally different marital situations for you. Clerice and Paul had spent ten years *anxiously* exchanging barbs, whereas Sharon and John had spent eighteen years *calmly* drifting. The differences in these two marital situations are obvious and glaring. My intent at this point, however, is to underscore a very important similarity having major significance—although neither couple realized it, they both were actually bringing two problems to the counseling session.

The first problem (and obviously why couples seek counseling) was that of a *deteriorating marital relationship*. Some of the more common descriptions of deterioration which I hear are these:

- having problems communicating
- marital conflict
- want to work on the relationship
- marital problems
- marital stress

At times, couples have difficulty identifying exactly what the problem is. But even in these instances, one thing is certain—they all realize that something is terribly wrong in their marriage. They know that the relationship has deteriorated.

It is this first problem—this deteriorated relationship—which tends to catch the helper's eye. Whether the helper is a counselor, pastor, or just a friend, we tend to want to focus on this first problem. We want to analyze . . . to figure out exactly what went wrong . . . to determine what needs to be corrected. We want to offer corrective advice. We believe that, once good advice is given, all that has to happen for improvement to be noted is for the necessary changes to be implemented. If the mates will just do what is right, then everything will work out satisfactorily.

This all sounds logical enough. What could be simpler than

doing what you ought to do? Unfortunately, the problem with this line of reasoning is that not all couples will do what they ought to. Although unhappy with the way things are and desiring things to be better, they appear to be helpless when it comes to making any adaptive changes which might result in an improvement in the marriage. Why is this?

Basically, the reason couples are often unable to constructively work on their marital relationship is a second problem they have . . . a problem which they also bring to counseling . . . but a problem of which they are largely unaware. I refer to this second problem as the problem of *polarization* or, stated more simply, just being "pushed to extremes." Being pushed to extremes, they are unwilling to do what they ought to in order to improve the marriage.

Polarization is an excellent term for describing this marital condition. As a scientific term, pertaining to electricity, the following partial definition may be helpful:

1. division into two opposites;
2. concentration about opposing extremes of interests on a continuum.

Sometimes mates become polarized in regard to their marital relationship. Pushed to extremes, they plant their feet, as it were, in blocks of concrete on opposite ends of the marriage. They become so strongly entrenched in their respective positions that they will not be moved. These are not positions in which they began the marital journey but they are destinations at which they have arrived and deviation from these spots is difficult.

The particular attributes which characterize polarization will be thoroughly discussed later. However, so you can get a feel for what we are talking about, let's look back at the two couples described earlier in this chapter. Both of these couples were polarized. Pushed to extremes, each mate saw the other as the problem. It was the other mate who was wrong. It was the other mate who needed to change. It was the other mate who deserved the blame for the marital deterioration. "My anger is justified . . . he hurt me." They were polarized. Are you beginning to get a feel for this second problem?

When mates are polarized, cooperation is nonexistent. They are angry and feel justified in their resistance to one another. The anger and resentment brought to the session by both of the mates stands in the way of any constructive change occurring. Being pushed to extremes in this manner is a far more pressing complication for a counselor than the problem of the deteriorated relationship.

Now, I am not trying to imply that the relationship is not of the utmost importance. Undoubtedly, it is. But the relationship problem is one which lends itself to fairly routine clinical work. We generally know how to treat anxious marriages like that of Clerice and Paul. And we know how to deal with drifting marriages like that of Sharon and John. But getting to the point where we can begin working on the marital relationship is another matter. In order to get at the relationship, we first have to get past the polarization.

For both of these couples, the more immediate problem was the problem of their polarization. They were pushed to extremes. You cannot work on the problem of the marriage until you first deal with the problem of polarization. Until the anger subsides and the blaming stops, any attempts at improving the marriage are futile. They only create greater frustration. Until the couple resolves their polarization and moves in from their opposite positions, they are not ready to work on the marriage. *Readiness* is a key word here. A couple has to be ready to work on their relationship. Unfortunately, some couples never become ready.

The Characteristics of Polarization

Being pushed to extremes, or polarized, is a complex concept. Only by focusing upon polarization in detail do we begin to recognize the four unique components or characteristics which work together to form this relational blight . . . characteristics which are held in common by all who are polarized.

I am not referring to demographic characteristics like race, creed, or socioeconomic status. These are not the characteristics held in common by the polarized. Unfortunately, no sociological group is exempt from this contributor to marital failure. Rather, the characteristics held in common by the polarized cross these artificial barriers. They are much more universal. The characteristics held in common by the polarized are their similarities in attitude and behavior.

Self-righteousness. The cornerstone of polarization is the pervasive attitude of self-righteousness which emanates from those couples who are pushed to extremes. Polarized mates always perceive themselves as right. They have done no wrong. They have done their best. They are the sinless ones.

To prove their respective rightness, they come with long lists of laurels and credits. With rationale after rationale, they offer examples of all of the things they have done in an effort to make the marriage work. They have tried. They have given. They have gone the extra mile. All of their efforts were futile. All of their attempts were in vain. They do not know what else to do.

Occasionally, a polarized mate will admit to being at least partially responsible for the marital deterioration:

> I know it takes two to make a marriage work. And even though I've tried my best, I know that I probably haven't always done everything the way I should have. I know I probably could have done better and, to some degree, am also responsible for what is happening in our marriage. *But . . .*

This entire monologue is nothing more than a smoke screen. Its intent is to soften the appearance of self-righteousness, which is so obviously present in the marriage. When mates begin to talk like this, I seldom believe what is being stated. Why should I? The individual making the statement doesn't even believe it. Generally, the least amount of challenging will result in the mate's taking a more honest position . . . one reaffirming his rightness.

Self-righteously, each clings to a position of rightness within the relationship. Each has done his or her best. Each is blameless. Neither admits to having done any wrong. And upon this foundation, the rest of the metaphorical fortress is built.

Justification.   The second major characteristic of polarization is the attitude of justification. Mates who are polarized not only believe that they have *done* right but also that they are *in* the right. They believe that their position, whatever it may be, is warranted. They are justified. They believe this because of what the other person has done *to* them. It is the mate who has messed up, who committed the wrong, who has not done his part. "And because he did [didn't], I am justified in feeling and behaving the way I do."

Polarized mates usually cite one of three rationales as justification for their position. The first justification for being polarized is that of being *wronged*:

"I am the one who has been wronged."

"I am the one who has been offended."

"I am the injured party."

"He hurt me!"

This rationale is most clearly illustrated in Sharon and John's case study. In that example, Sharon believed that she had been wronged by John. It was he who had performed the dastardly deed. He had developed a relationship with another woman. His actions had hurt her deeply and with this hurt came a great deal of intense anger. He had committed the offense. And because of his indiscretion, Sharon's polarization was justified. She was in the right.

A second justification for being polarized is that of being *frustrated*:

"I've tried and worked for years . . . now I'm fed up!"

"I'm tired of trying."

"I've given and given but he's never responded."

"I've tried to meet her needs, but it's never been enough. Now I'm through trying."

Clerice and Paul provide the clearest example of this rationale of justification. In that case illustration, both mates claimed to be frustrated. They were frustrated by the behavior of the other mate. Both saw themselves as having done the right things . . . making all the valiant efforts. If only the other mate had responded appropriately, things could have been different. If only Paul had been willing to lay aside some of his personal preoccupations and given more of himself to the marriage, Clerice would not have been nearly as frustrated. If only Clerice could have been less demanding. If only she could have backed off some, Paul would not have been nearly as frustrated.

Clerice and Paul each saw the other's behavior as a direct rejection of acknowledged needs . . . and this was frustrating. Similar to being wronged, being frustrated prompted an intense emotional response. Both were angry . . . and both were justified. Both were in the right.

The final justification for being polarized is that of *piety*:

"It was her duty, but she failed."

"He had an obligation, but he 'blew it.' "

"She hasn't met her wifely responsibilities."

"He never would fulfill his husbandly role."

Piety typically focuses upon rules and roles. Every marriage has rules and each mate has a belief about what the roles of husband and wife ought to be. "She never loved me the way she should have." "He never was the spiritual leader in the home as he should have been." When a mate fails to "measure up" to these prescribed rules and roles, the other mate often feels piously justified in taking a polarized stance.

This justification of piety is best illustrated with Sharon and John. Sharon's justification was based on her belief that John had wronged her through his involvement with another woman. From John's perspective, however, Sharon had failed in her responsibilities as a wife.

On numerous occasions throughout the duration of the marriage, John had approached Sharon in an attempt to develop a more intimate relationship. And time after time, with one excuse or another, Sharon had discounted his attempts. "Had she only responded in the way in which she should have, I wouldn't have been forced to turn to someone else for 'friendship.' " Now, John did not state his justification quite this plainly at the first counseling session. He was too intimidated by Sharon's emotional condition to be so bold. Nevertheless, this was his position. And as counseling progressed, both his belief of justification and position of polarization became strikingly more apparent. He too was "in the right."

Blaming. The third major characteristic of polarization is the tendency to blame the other mate for the marital difficulties. Although blaming could be an attitude, it is also a behavior. It is something we *do* to someone else. For polarized mates, frequent verbal attacks, placing the blame for the marital failure on the other spouse, are common occurrences.

The examples listed above are meant to illustrate some of the more common expressions of blaming utilized by polarized mates. Sometimes the mates become much more specific about what has been wrongly done. But the theme is always the same: "It is your fault." It is *always* the other mate's fault and the polarized spouse is more than willing to make this fact well known.

Once again, the two case studies already mentioned provide clear examples of the blaming characteristic of polarization. Clerice would blame Paul with the following accusation:

"You are selfish. Take, take, take . . . that's all you ever did. You never gave me anything!"

Paul would blame Clerice with the following accusation:

"Complain, complain, complain . . . I could never do enough. No matter how much I gave, you always wanted more. You wanted too much!"

Sharon would blame John with the following accusation:

"You betrayed me. You became involved with another woman!"

John would blame Sharon with the following accusation:

"You failed me. You reneged on your responsibility as a wife!"

The failing nature of these marriages was never in question. Failure was readily admitted to by all concerned. But each spouse blamed their mate for the failure. And that blaming behavior is characteristic of polarization.

Resistance. The final characteristic of polarization is resistance. When combined with self-righteousness, justification, and blaming, resistance completes the whole of polarization. Much like blaming, resistance is also capable of being both an attitude and a behavior. Within marital polarization, it is the behavioral nature of resistance which presents us the most difficulty.

Resistance is the single most problematic characteristic of polar- ization ever faced by a counselor. Resistance prevents change. It maintains things as they are. It keeps the couple locked into their self-defeating interactional patterns. In the height of resistance, both mates absolutely refuse to change their respective positions. Each mate wants things to be different . . . to be improved. Neither of them likes the conflict . . . the marital strain. But neither one of

them is willing to make any constructive changes in order to bring this about. Neither one will make a move . . . whether it be the first or the last.

To "not change" is the goal of resistance. From their polarized positions, each mate will resist personal change at all costs. Why should they change? They are the righteous ones. They are the mates who are justified in their position. The other mate is the one to be blamed. Therefore, why should they change? Determined, resolute, oppositional . . . with feet firmly set in concrete . . . they will not be moved.

I received a telephone call one day from a pastor which illustrates this particular characteristic of polarization. He wanted to refer a couple to me with whom he had been counseling. He had seen them on and off for approximately one year. During that period of time, he had done everything he knew to do with them but nothing had changed:

> I've counseled with him individually, with her individually, and with both of them together. I've told them what they need to do in order to get along better with each other and to have the marriage God wants them to have. But things haven't gotten any better. They just don't seem to be able to cooperate with one another and do what they ought to.

The pastor was stumped. In utter frustration, he had decided it was best to refer this couple to someone else for counseling.

I was not present during the counseling sessions which he had conducted so I am uncertain of all the advice that was given to the couple. But in the time spent on the telephone with the pastor, it appeared as though he had made some good suggestions. Had the couple followed his admonitions, their marriage might have improved. But they didn't . . . and it didn't.

The pastor's frustration stemmed largely from his failure to

accurately assess what was going on. He saw the deteriorated relationship plainly enough. But he did not understand polarization and, in this instance, the particular characteristic of resistance which so controlled the couple's relationship. With an appropriate understanding of polarization, the pastor would not have been perplexed with the couple's behavior. The foot-dragging, the excuses, the incompleted tasks . . . all of this would have made sense. Had he understood polarization, (1) he would not have been confused, (2) he would not have been nearly as frustrated, and (3) he would not have counseled them as he did. But he did not recognize this additional problem. So as he worked on the relationship, the couple continued to relate to one another in self-defeating manners. Relationally stuck, they continued in their resistant behavior.

In an effort at summarizing this section, let me restate that the four characteristics just described work together to form the problem of polarization. Couples who are pushed to extremes do not possess only one of these characteristics. They possess them all. Mates who are polarized:

1. believe that they are "sinless" when it comes to the marriage . . . they have done no wrong (self-righteous);
2. believe that their mate has in some way committed the wrong which has led to the marital deterioration (justification);
3. actively make the villainous mate aware of his failure (blaming); and
4. actively resist any form of personal change in regard to the relationship (resistance).

With the problem of polarization, is there any wonder some marriages just don't seem to get any better?

The Inadequacies of Marital Polarization

Marital polarization is routinely a problem for those who seek counseling. However, it can also be a painfully present enigma in

marriages which, for the time being, are more stable and healthy
. . . in couples who are not found on any counselor's list of clientele
. . . in marriages like yours and mine. But if this relational blight is
allowed to persist in an otherwise healthy marriage, it can maneuver
what appears to be a stable relationship to the brink of instability.
And the time required to accomplish the transformation need not be
long in duration.

Pam came for counseling in the midst of an emotional crisis.
Tom, her husband for eleven years, had just filed for divorce.
Shocked and confused, Pam found it difficult to believe that the
conflict between the two of them had come this far. She described
the first half of her marriage with Tom as good. For five years they
had enjoyed each other's company and invested both time and
energy into the relationship. Then came Sarah, their first child.
The adjustments necessitated by parenthood seemed especially
difficult for them. Tom claimed he wasn't getting enough attention.
Pam countered with the claim that she wasn't getting enough
assistance. With these initial accusations, the battle lines were
drawn and they actively began to resist one another.

The polarization quickly spread to every area of their marital life.
Even the smallest issue became an opportunity to demonstrate
noncooperativeness:

> The last five years have been a total disaster. I guess we're
> both weary of the incessant bickering and fighting. It is as
> though we got into a vicious cycle and couldn't get out. I
> guess Tom has finally found a way to end it.

The story of Pam and Tom demonstrates the destructive nature of
polarization. They did not start out pushed to extremes, but when
they began to resist one another, they found it difficult to stop. They
would not reason. They would not talk. They would not cooperate.
With one arbitrary move after another, they maintained an emo-

tional distance that was devastating to the relationship. Non-cooperative . . . locked in a vicious cycle . . . unable to stop . . . they finally ended their pain.

Regardless of the particular situation, marital polarization is never warranted. Whether it be with problematic marriages like those of Pam and Tom, Clerice and Paul, or Sharon and John . . . or whether it be with the less troubled marriages of those a little closer to home (yours and mine) . . . polarization is NEVER an appropriate spousal response. Never is:

- the pompous attitude of *self-righteousness,*
- the smugness of *justification,*
- the aggressiveness of *blaming,* or
- the blatant noncooperativeness of *resistance*

ever warranted in a marriage.

The use of "never" and "ever" underscores the importance of the point that, no matter how severely we may believe that we have been wronged, polarization is never an acceptable way for us to respond to one another. To support my assertion regarding the inappropriateness of marital polarization are the following three observations:

Observation #1. Polarization within marriage is never helpful. Think back to the last time when being self-righteous, justified, blaming, and resistant helped your marital relationship. If you are being honest, you will probably remember a time when you behaved in this manner. And if you are being totally honest, you will also remember that it did not help things very much.

It's not difficult to understand why polarization doesn't help. Do you know anyone who responds positively to being blamed . . . to being told that he is at fault? Do you like to deal with someone who, after blaming you for something which you have supposedly done, stoically and pompously refuses to make any constructive effort toward working things out? The counterproductivity of this kind of behavior is plain to see.

Polarization never helps . . . it always makes thing worse. It totally works at cross-purposes with the goal of developing an intimate and close marital relationship. It maintains emotional distance between mates and, by so doing, encourages a marriage to drift. This counterproductivity alone would be sufficient reason to disavow the appropriateness of polarization. Yet there are two other reasons which further support my contention.

Observation #2.   Polarization within marriage is seldom based on an accurate assessment of the relationship.

As I have already stated, self-righteousness, or the attitude that you are the sinless one in the relationship, is the cornerstone of polarization. When you add to self-righteousness the justification that your mate is the culprit and in the wrong, you are left with a dynamic duo of a belief system which defies reason. Seldom do these two estimations of the relationship represent an accurate assessment of the situation.

Marriages are interpersonal relationships involving two individuals. Within marriage, there are no villains . . . and there are no heroes. No mate is totally a sinner . . . and no mate is totally a saint. Occasionally we do have mates who come close to approximating one of these two extremes but generally, no one wears a black hat and no one wears a white hat. Rather, both mates wear hats a little grey in color. A more accurate description would be a marriage built on cooperative effort with each mate having a role to fulfill . . . a part to play . . . for good and for bad.

To base polarization on attitudes of personal sinlessness and spousal guilt, therefore, is equivalent to building a house on sand. It is to erect a rationale on an unsure foundation . . . albeit, an illusion. The one who blames has also had a part in the deterioration of the relationship. The one who piously resists has also contributed to the marital failure. But this realization is seldom recognized by those who are polarized, and this lack of recognition is precisely the problem.

Once mates who are pushed to extremes begin to recognize their own contribution to the marital strain . . . that they, too, are at fault . . . and that they, too, can be blamed . . . it becomes difficult for them to maintain their polarized position. It is difficult to be nonforgiving when you, too, are in need of forgiveness. As mates begin to realize this, they begin to soften. Until they realize their own involvement in the marital failure, the polarization will persist. Until each mate accepts his own personal guilt, little progress will be made.

As mates genuinely accept ownership of the fact that they, too, are at least in part responsible for their present dilemma, change begins to take place. As the attitudes of self-righteousness begin to erode, the resistance and uncooperation which has kept the couple caught in a vicious cycle begins to give way to more conciliatory gestures. As each mate begins accepting personal responsibility for his own nonconstructive behavior—past, present, and future—each becomes willing to stop the blaming and start the helping. It is then, and only then, that true working on the relationship can begin.

Observation #3.   Polarization within marriage *is never Christian behavior.*

The Bible has a great deal of instruction regarding our conduct toward one another. We are told to do many things but never are we told to be polarized. Never are we told:

- to be **self-righteous,**
- to be **justified,**
- to be **blaming,** or
- to be **resistant.**

Quite the contrary, the biblical imperatives are for Christians:

- to love one another (1 Corinthians 13:13),
- to show mercy (Matthew 5:7),
- to be forbearing (Colossians 3:13),
- to be slow to anger (James 1:19), and
- to be nonoffensive (1 Peter 4:15).

These biblical imperatives are clearly contradictory of the characteristics of polarization described earlier. And so they should be. Nowhere in the life of a Christian is there room for polarization. This is true in any relationship . . . and especially marriage. Even in times when we can honestly claim to have done the right . . . and even in times when we can accurately assess to have been wronged . . . it is never our role to offer blame or resistance. The Christian has a high calling and with this calling is an aspiration to a more perfect behavior.

Above all else, Christians are a *forgiving* people. The importance placed on forgiveness by Jesus is easily recognized. One of the more familiar passages illustrating His views is that recorded by Matthew. In a discourse between Jesus and Peter, Matthew records:

> Then Peter came up and asked him, "Lord, how often am I to forgive my brother if he goes on wronging me? As many as seven times?" Jesus replied, "I do not say seven times, I say seventy times seven."

Matthew 18:21, 22

This issue of forgiveness is an area that I will deal with in greater detail later in this book. Suffice it to say at this time, however, that Jesus saw forgiveness as a critical Christian characteristic. It was not optional equipment. It was standard. Jesus' alluding to "seventy times seven" was not an attempt at establishing a more righteous goal for us to strive for. Neither was He suggesting that we all become junior accountants and keep more accurate count of the alleged misdeeds perpetrated against us. Rather, it was an admonition that we do not keep count at all. As a good friend recently shared with me, "Jesus was not extending the limits . . . He was eliminating them." And that is exactly what He did.

Forgiveness is a wonderful thing to experience . . . as either the forgiver or the forgivee. As recipients of forgiveness, Christians should realize this better than anyone else. It is healing. It is restoring. It is reuniting. But more than being wonderful, it is a command. It is something which we are supposed to do.

Forgiveness is a differentiating element . . . a characteristic which distinguishes the Christian from the non-Christian. It is how we are known. Unfortunately for some marriages, that which is *supposed* to occur is far different from that which actually *does* occur. For some Christian couples, forgiveness is a nonexistent element. All too often, these couples act as if marriage is exempted from the forgiveness requirement. And in most of these marriages, the relationship sadly reflects the deficit.

Where there is polarization, there is no forgiveness. Without forgiveness, couples are stuck in their misery. Without forgiveness, marriages deteriorate. And without forgiveness, behavior ceases to be Christian. Is there any question as to why I say polarization is never warranted?

I have found that, as couples are able to extend to one another the same forgiveness which they themselves have received through Jesus Christ, wonderful things happen within marriages. In troubled marriages, forgiveness is a prerequisite to true marital renewal. For the rest of us, it is a necessary ingredient for the development of intimacy. Regardless of our marital condition, forgiveness is Christian; polarization is not.

What You Can Do

Marital polarization (self-righteousness, justification, blaming, and resistance) is never acceptable behavior within a relationship. It is nonproductive, seldom accurate, and never Christian. Whether as a persistent form of interacting *or* an occasional way of responding, polarization is destructive in nature. As long as you allow yourselves to become pushed to extremes, and thus, to assume polarized positions, little positive gain can be expected in your marriage.

With the destructive nature of polarization in mind, I have developed a brief Polarization Checklist for your use when you are angry with your mate. It is hoped that, through the utilization of this checklist, the grip which polarization holds on some relationships will be reduced.

Polarization Checklist

1. What has your mate done to upset you?
2. How have *you* contributed to this situation?
3. Are you *totally* blameless?
4. Do you have the right to feel totally righteous in this situation?
5. How have you responded toward your mate regarding this situation?
6. What have you said to your mate about this situation?
7. How would you like for things to be between the two of you right now?
8. Is how you are currently behaving toward your mate helping your relationship?
9. Is how you are currently behaving toward your mate based on totally accurate information?
10. Is how you are currently behaving toward your mate Christian?
11. If you were going to be cooperative with your mate, what would you do differently from what you are currently doing?
12. What is stopping you from being cooperative?

The Polarization Checklist reflects much of what has been stated throughout this chapter. To defuse the power and prevalence of polarization, we have to recognize both the fallacy of thought upon which it is built and the inadequacy of the behavior which maintains it.

In marital relationships, *few* of us are ever totally sinless . . . and *none* of us ever has the right to cling to our own self-righteousness. Our responsibility is always one of behaving constructively . . . not destructively. There is no place for blame and resistance . . . only forgiveness and cooperation.

As each of us (1) accepts responsibility for our own personal (mis)behavior, (2) stops the blaming, (3) extends forgiveness to our mate, and (4) begins to function in a cooperative manner, progress can be made in our marriage. In essence, this formula is the antidote for polarization. It will bring change. Without it, we will continue to drift toward destruction.

PART THREE

HOW TO PREVENT A DRIFTING MARRIAGE

— 9 —

CHRISTIAN
RESPONSIBILITIES

To speak of Christian responsibilities, as opposed to the responsibilities of mates in general, is an act of differentiation. It establishes separateness, asserting the fact that there are differences between those who call themselves Christians and those who do not.

This concept of *difference* should really come as no surprise. There is no new revelation here. The Christian community has always seen itself as distinct and different from the non-Christian community. We even refer to those who are not Christian by specific names and terms. For instance, some of the more derogatory labels would include *sinners* and *heathen*. Kinder terms would include *secular* and *worldly*. Regardless of the names you prefer to use, however, the clear fact remains that there are recognized differences between those *within* and those *without* the realm of Christendom. Simply stated, having a personal relationship with Jesus Christ changes who we are and because we are changed, our behavior is also changed. Although conversion does not make anyone an automatic clone of Jesus, spiritual growth and maturity bring improved behavior.

Sometimes there is confusion regarding this attitude that Christians live a better quality of life than do non-Christians. This confusion is prompted by actually observing how some of us behave. None of us is perfect and it doesn't take long for the world to recognize that fact. "If he's a Christian, why does he behave as he does?"

I believe part of the confusion can be clarified by the following observation:

> There are some people who are better by personality than others are by grace.

I think we all can agree on this. There are non-Christians who are by nature very gracious people. They are kind, giving, and caring. We like to be around them. On the other hand, there are Christians who are ornery and obnoxious and whom we find difficult to like, much less love. Can you see the potential for confusion?

So, how do we put this all together? How do we make sense out of what appear to be contradictory facts? How can we uphold the belief that Christians live better lives than non-Christians, yet at the same time, admit that some non-Christians live better lives than do some Christians? I believe the apparent contradiction is dispelled when we begin to look at ourselves as individuals. Once we place our focus on each other as individuals having uniquely inherent capabilities and capacities, we can honestly say that it is only through a relationship with Christ that any of us can hope to approach our true potential.

In Christ there is completeness. Outside of Christ we remain fragmented. Regardless of our personal and natural goodness, without Christ it remains only a sampling of *what it could be*. The non-Christian who is good and gracious would be even more so with Christ in his life, and just imagine what the obnoxious Christian would be like if it were not for the influence of Christ. Undoubtedly, Jesus brings improvement to our human condition. He just has more work to do on some of us than He does on others.

This same reality can be said of marriages. There are marriages in the world which are healthy and stable. Contrarily, there are Christian marriages which are marginal at best. Yet the fact remains, even though there are secular marriages which are vibrant and thriving, these relationships are only a portion of what they could be. It is only in Christ that a marriage approaches its true potential.

As we can see, lives changed by Christ are distinctively different from those which are not. This is fact. It is a given. It is important. It is the most obvious of the differences which exist between Christian and non-Christian communities. Yet, as true as this difference in the quality of life may be, I want to focus on a less obvious difference. Rather than focusing on the quality of existence which naturally emanates from a life lived in consort with Christ, my goal is to identify the responsibilities which accompany such a union. For those of us who claim the name *Christian*, we also assume responsibilities.

Responsibilities

A book should be written entitled *Artificial Definitions*. In it we would discuss terms which mean one thing to the secular world, but an entirely different thing to the Christian. For example, *success* would be one such term. Whereas the secular world tends to measure success in the accumulation of wealth and status, success for the Christian has a more spiritual connotation. Rather than being determined by accumulation, it is directly related to our ability to seek and to find God's will for our lives. As a friend recently remarked, "Jesus' idea of success was the cross." Obviously, this is a drastically different view from that held by the secular world.

The need for such a book rests with the problem which often arises when we try to live a Christian life while operating under these artificial definitions. Trying to live a genuinely Christian life under the terms and conditions established by the world is frustrating and futile. As we learn to clearly understand the differences between the Christian and non-Christian definitions, we are better prepared to make appropriate choices.

Responsibility is a term which should be in this book. It elicits distinct feelings whenever it is heard, and these feelings are seldom ones of jubilation.

An experience I recently had at a pastor's retreat will illustrate this point. I wanted to discuss with the pastors on this retreat the differing views held toward responsibility. To introduce the topic, I used a word-association exercise. I gave them a word or phrase and asked that they respond with the kind of feelings which these prompted. Here is how it went:

TERM/PHRASE	ELICITED FEELINGS
warm, sunny beaches	calm, peaceful, relaxed, carefree
cloudy days	depressed, sad, lethargic
mother	love, safe, comfort, support
mother-in-law	mixed responses ranging from positive (love) to negative (criticized)
Saturday night	anxious, panic, pressured (Can you guess why?)
responsibility	work, drudgery, anxious, tired, overwhelmed, obligation

Look at their responses. How would you have responded to these phrases and terms? Your responses would probably have been fairly similar to theirs. I wasn't really interested in what kind of feelings were associated with warm, sunny beaches, cloudy days, etc. I only gave them the first five terms and phrases to get them loosened up.

What I was primarily interested in was their perception of responsibility. As you can see, they saw it as a "heavy" word. Again, their feelings regarding responsibility probably aren't much different from yours and mine.

We tend to perceive responsibility as a heavy word. It is hard and harsh. It is one which always entails work and effort. It demands. When used, we are required to do something. "Supposed to," "ought," "should". . . this is the language of responsibility. At least, this is how we perceive it.

My disagreement with how we perceive responsibility is not with the "supposed to," "ought," "should" aspect of the term. I believe that this is actually a very real part of the word. However, my contention rests more with our attitude toward this required aspect. We tend to view any form of obligation as extremely negative. Demands are terrible. Life would be so much easier if obligations were not placed upon us. Or at least, so we think.

The attitude held toward responsibility is what differentiates the Christian perspective from that of the secular world. This difference is what determines what is artificial and what is not. It is the secular world which tends to see responsibility as negative. The Christian's perspective, on the other hand, is a more positive one because it is God who establishes our responsibilities. It is He who determines what we "are supposed to," "ought to," and "should" do. And, most importantly, He is not arbitrary.

To view responsibilities negatively is to deny the goodness of God and cast Him as an arbitrary dictator whose intent is to make us unhappy. How much further from the truth can this perspective be? God always has our best interests at heart. Anything He tells us to do is for our ultimate good. We may not understand it. Neither may we particularly realize the benefit in the present. But our best interest is always the goal of God's commands. He is not arbitrary.

For the Christian, therefore, responsibility is a way of life. There is clear direction. Little is left to confused contemplation. Sought, bought, and taught, we, too, like Paul, "press for the mark." With a well-developed, responsible nature, we do what we ought to do . . . or at least, we try to. It is demanding. It requires effort. And it is work. But we benefit accordingly. God is not arbitrary.

Christians who try to live under the world's artificial definition—who see responsibilities as negative—try to live as close to the edge as possible. How little can I give and still be considered Christian? How much can I be *in* the world before I am *of* the world? How can I dodge what I am "supposed" to do and still be okay?

I see this attitude in some of the clients with whom I work. It really speaks to the issue of spirituality or, more importantly, the lack thereof. This attitude really concerns me, not totally from the standpoint of whether they have finally skirted over the edge, but rather, from all of the good things which they will miss. In perceiving God's commands as arbitrary and trying to find satisfaction by denying responsibilities, they only succeed in missing His blessings. Again, God is **not** arbitrary.

Those who live according to the standards of the secular world find few things which either "are supposed to," "ought," or "should" be done. Little is required and nothing is sacred. We are hard pressed to develop a list of responsibilities. Within the secular world, there is no absolute authority to which to look for direction. The best that can be acknowledged is the legal system which directs its energies at negatives and dwells on extremes. For example, under the legal directives, I am not required to be a good neighbor. I am only prohibited from being a bad one. Within the world, to hate and snub my neighbor is allowable behavior. I begin to be held responsible only when I harm him. How different this is from the responsibility of the Christian who is to love his neighbor.

By claiming to be Christian, there are responsibilities associated with that claim that are not required of the world. These responsibilities emanate from the biblical standard. This is not to say that non-Christians cannot assume these responsibilities, that they cannot perform them, or even that they cannot benefit from them. We know that non-Christians can live good, moral lives. We also know that following God's directives, even when being non-Christian, will result in a better quality of life. However, what is *optional* for the world is *requisite* for Christians. We are supposed to do some things which our secular brethren are not.

Christians, fortunately, never have to speak of responsibility without also speaking of power. The Lord does not guide His people in any direction in which He does not also provide for their needs. Although the responsibility is ours, the power is His. He is more than willing to endow us with whatever it is that we need to both be what He wants us to be and do what He wants us to do.

Jan and I both like meaningful sayings. One which hangs in our kitchen serves to remind us of Christ's primacy in our lives. It is this:

God is ready to assume full responsibility for the life wholly yielded to Him.

As individuals and as a couple, this has been our testimony. Through the years, we have accomplished many things. But whether the accomplishment is in what we've been able to do for others or what we've been able to do within our marriage, there is nothing for which we can boast. It is the Lord who has always given us the power to do that for which He holds us responsible. He has never failed us.

In times of difficulty, He gives strength. In times of disappointment, He gives comfort. And in times of hesitancy, when we wonder what to do (or, when knowing what to do, we wonder if it is worth it all), He gives direction and power. This is a power which the world knows nothing about and sadly lacks. Truly, the Lord makes a difference in the lives of His people.

Christian Responsibilities in Marriage

The theme of Christian responsibilities is no more evident than in the area of marriage. Again, when contrasted with our secular counterparts, we find that there are requirements which accompany the claim of being Christian. Although I would be quite reticent to cite any formally accepted responsibilities in the realm of secular marriage, I have no such hesitancy in identifying what I believe to be some of the "oughts" for Christians.

In my opinion, we as Christian mates have two primary responsibilities within our marriages. The first of these is that *we love our mates*. The second is that *we esteem them*. The next two chapters will be devoted to clearly explaining each of these primary Christian responsibilities. Hopefully, with greater understanding, there will be greater application.

Before launching into an explanation of how we love and esteem our mates, I want to close this chapter with thoughts about drifting and its prevention. First, drifting has never been God's design for marriage. It has been easy for me to reach this conclusion. Quite simply, a *drifting* marriage is a *failing* marriage . . . and it has never been God's plan for marriages to fail. Rather, it is His plan that they succeed. Marriage is intended to be a mutually satisfying and enriching relationship. Anything short of this deviates from God's plan. And drifting definitely qualifies as a deviation.

My final thought is in reference to the emphasis on prevention. After all, preventing drifting marriages is the focus of this final section. Since I spent most of this book identifying how we do it *wrong*, the least I can do is to spend a couple of chapters on how to do it *right*. When we do what is right—when we do what we are supposed to do—we prevent our marriage from drifting. Doing what is right, therefore, is preventative.

It's really quite simple. All that it takes for us to have a successful marriage is to fulfill our Christian responsibilities. As we love and esteem our mates . . . as we fulfill our marital responsibilities . . . as we do what we ought to do . . . we achieve what God intended for marriage to be. Avoiding our responsibilities will only lead to failure, whether through drifting or another form. Being responsible obviously has its benefits.

— 10 —
LOVING
YOUR
MATE

Referring to love as a responsibility may appear somewhat odd, especially to those who are unfamiliar with a Christian perspective. This is not surprising. Many of the views broadly held by Christians often appear odd to those of the secular world. The suggestion that love is a responsibility may prompt questions like these:

Isn't love spontaneous?

Isn't it something which either happens or fails to happen?

How do you make something like love a responsibility?

Much of this confusion stems from our (mis)understanding of what love is.

The secular world places an emphasis upon the emotional dimension of love. With an eye toward the pleasurable, love is viewed as something to be felt. It is an emotional high. It is to be savored. We have difficulty describing how love comes. It is nebulous and difficult to explain. Like the wind, it seems to uncontrollably come and go. It often appears to be accidental. Much like walking beside a hole in the ground, love can be fallen into . . . and just as easily fallen out of. But though it is difficult to explain, we know that when it is present, emotions are in full swing. They are pushed to extremes. *Giddy, excited, obsessed* . . . these are terms which aptly describe how it feels to be in love . . . and it feels good.

The emotional quality of love is both rewarding and important.

There is no denying this fact. Yet, to be enamored solely with the emotional aspect of love, to the exclusion of any other quality, is a grave error. For love is more than mere feelings alone. It is multidimensional. There is more to love than just the single dimension of feelings. In addition to the emotional dimension, love is also behavioral. By this I mean that love is also expressed and demonstrated. And it is with the recognition of the behavioral dimension of love that the distinction between the Christian and non-Christian realms becomes apparent.

Love actually encompasses two dimensions. There is the dimension of *being in love* (emotional) and there is the dimension of *behaving in love* (behavioral). These are two distinctly different entities. And whereas the world tends to endorse the first of these two dimensions as its perspective of what love is, Christendom advances a view which includes them both.

For a Christian to *be* in love, he is also supposed to *behave* in love. And it is the Christian's inclusion of the behavioral aspect of love, or the acceptance of this fuller definition, which erects love as a responsibility. For even though feelings can fluctuate seemingly regardless of our intent, behaviors are far more within our control. And with the acceptance of this total definition comes the responsibility for Christian mates to demonstrate their love toward one another.

As you can see, love is much more than giddy feelings and pleasurable experiences. Whereas this distinction of difference may have little implication for the secular, it is of immense importance to the Christian. Within the realm of Christendom, the "more" computes to responsibility. For the Christian, merely being in love is not enough. Christian mates also have the responsibility of behaving in love . . . and this distinguishes them from the world.

In order to gain a better understanding of the breadth of this responsibility, I now intend to identify some of the characteristics of behaving in love. How do we go about demonstrating our love for our mate? Let's see.

Behaving in Love

As a marriage counselor, I have the opportunity to become familiar with a great many troubled relationships. The presenting problem will often vary from one marriage to the next. But the general condition of these relationships is usually the same: failing.

In responding to the many and diverse situations which are brought to counseling, there are a few questions which I tend to ask each of the couples in the first session. One of these routine questions is this: "What is it that is keeping the two of you together?"

As you might surmise, I have heard about every response imaginable to this inquiry. Some of the more frequent replies are:

"We are staying together for the sake of the children."

"Neither of us believes in divorce."

"We don't like the idea of 'giving up' on anything."

"Neither of us could make it financially on our own."

Although these are common responses, there is one which surpasses these in its frequency of use. Whether used by itself or as an adjunct to one of those listed above, the most frequently cited reason for a couple's remaining together is this: "We love each other."

On occasion, I find this response totally humorous. After both observing a couple's interaction within a counseling session and then listening to the stories of (mis)deeds and events which make up their marital history, I often sit in utter amazement as they actually recite the words: "We love each other." From what I have observed and heard, there has been little demonstration of this love toward one another . . . either in the present or in the past.

Occasionally I am tempted to ask how they think a husband or wife who is in love acts toward a mate. But I usually refrain from such a maneuver until I get to know the couple better. Still, the discrepancy between what is stated and what is actually done continues to amaze me.

I am not so naive as to think that mates will always do what they ought to do . . . that they will always behave in love in addition to being in love. But I do believe, at least for the sake of the marriage, that the majority of their efforts need to be toward that end. And this is true for all marriages . . . not just those seen in counseling offices.

I am sure that the troubled relationships seen by counselors are not the only marriages where mates, while possibly being in love, are failing to behave in love. None of us is immune from the possibility of failure in this regard, but neither are we exempted from the responsibility.

Let's bring behaving in love down to where we live . . . to your marriage and mine. How do we fulfill our Christian responsibility to behaving in love? In a practical sense, I believe the following four characteristics must be demonstrated: respect, honesty, forgiveness, and commitment. These are all vital to the growth of a quality relationship. If these four characteristics are present in a marriage, then we are behaving in love. If they are absent, then we are not. It's as simple as that.

Respect

Respect is most frequently thought of in its attitudinal form. We all know what it is to think highly of an individual . . . to admire him or to have confidence in her. Within marriage, this is an important consideration. In fact, it is so important that I seriously doubt whether love for a mate can long exist in a relationship where an attitude of respect is absent. Without respect there is no love. But as important as this attitudinal element may be, respect is also a loving behavior. And there are several ways in which you extend respect toward your mate.

Be Considerate.   One way to demonstrate respect is by being considerate. Being considerate requires the giving of special attention to your mate. It is exhibited by patience as opposed to impatience. It is the extension of kindness, or an agreeable and friendly nature, instead of unkind deeds. One wife complained to me that her husband seemed to take every opportunity available to him to verbally "spit" on her. The incidents she cited were definitely examples of unkind behavior and, in turn, a lack of consideration. The frequency of his verbal attacks greatly damaged the quality of their relationship.

Rudeness, abruptness, embarrassing actions . . . whether in public or in private, are always detrimental and act as further examples of inconsiderate and nonloving behavior. How much more could be gained through common courtesy.

Another example of consideration is empathy or, in a marital sense, trying to see your mate's point of view. It is amazing to see the positive ramifications which come from placing yourself in your mate's position. Trying to experience his feelings or her beliefs can greatly influence how you respond to one another. It often allows opportunities for genuine understanding and the extension of emotional support. All of this is simply the result of displaying a little consideration.

Be Giving.   A second way to demonstrate respect is to be giving. By giving, I am referring to the recognizing, acknowledging, and attending to the legitimate needs of a mate. If the concept of giving were placed on a continuum, we would find its opposite end points to be too giving and not giving enough. A wife who waits on her husband hand and foot would be an example of the too-giving end of the continuum, whereas a husband who never gives at all would be an example of not giving enough.

As with most characteristics or concepts, there is a balance to be struck. Either too much or too little of a good thing can be damaging. As you move toward the center from either end of this continuum, you will find a range which works best in marriage.

A familiar term for the not-giving-enough end of the continuum is *selfish*. Selfishness is marked by a clear statement to the effect that "all that matters is what I want." Those mates who behave selfishly are takers as opposed to givers, and regardless of the amount of lip service a taker may give to the claim of being in love, selfishness definitely fails as a demonstration of behaving in love.

Allow Personal Responsibility. A third way whereby respect is demonstrated is by allowing personal responsibility. Sometimes we mistakenly view our mately roles as that of being "protectors" as opposed to helpers. One example of this would be the overzealous solving of your mate's problem. Jumping in and solving his problem, although having the appearance of being a good thing to do, can be detrimental to his personal growth. This form of rescuing not only interferes with his development of independence, it also suggests a lack of respect for his competency.

Craig and Elaine offer us a clear example of what failing to allow your mate to be responsible for himself can do. Craig had already filed for divorce when they came to the first session. He made it perfectly clear that his only reason for being present was Elaine's insistence.

Elaine was obviously nervous. In fact, frantic would probably be a better description. Craig, on the other hand, was calm. Was he cold and callous? Did he have no feelings at all? Did it not bother him that his wife was depressed and distraught? In short, Craig responded that he cared very much for Elaine. But he valued his sanity above their relationship:

I've got to get free of her control. We've been married eight years and I've yet to find anything that I do right. My manners aren't appropriate. I have poor taste in clothes. I can't even talk right. Elaine has spent eight years trying to "make me better."

I'm very successful in what I do. But that doesn't seem to make any difference to Elaine. So what if I occasionally wear an open collar instead of a tie. Who cares? I've told her that these are just differences in opinion over things that don't mean much. She just needs to let me be me. I'm not going to embarrass her. But that doesn't change a thing. She keeps on correcting me.

I love Elaine. I just can't live with her. I don't feel good about myself anymore. My confidence has declined. I've just got to get free of her control and figure out who I am again. I can't do it in the marriage.

Throughout eight years of marriage, Elaine constantly crossed Craig's personal boundaries. She constantly took on his problems as her problems. Whether in the business world, where she told him what decisions he should make, or in the lesser areas of dress and speech, Craig felt totally out of control. He felt like a failure. Ultimately, he ended his pain by getting a divorce, freeing himself from Elaine's control.

Another way in which we fail to allow personal responsibility is in the area of feelings. We notoriously fail to share concerns, complaints, and criticisms because of the fear that our mates could not handle it.

"I don't want to hurt his feelings."

"I don't want to make her depressed."

Quite frankly, I believe there are very few things which people cannot handle. But shielding your mate in this manner, although

191

having the appearance of good, always precipitates worse circumstances. It clearly demonstrates an attitude of noncompetency toward him or her.

By allowing your mate to be responsible for his own problems and feelings, you allow him to develop individual competency. Well-intended overprotection, whether through rescuing or shielding, demonstrates a lack of respect for him. Instead, if you really love him, you need to demonstrate your confidence in his abilities by allowing the acceptance of personal responsibility.

Accept Your Mate's Uniqueness. Another way in which respect is demonstrated is by accepting your mate's uniqueness. My wife and I have many similarities. Likewise, there are many ways in which we are different. I imagine it is much the same with you and your mate. One of our differences is in our social dispositions. Simply stated, she is social and I am not. Jan loves the church get-togethers and the office parties. I endure them. Now, I am not antisocial. Rather, I prefer to think of myself as just being nonsocial. My preferred social group is a size of one or two as opposed to mass.

This difference in our social dispositions could become a problem for us, if we allowed it. If Jan took the position that she was right and I was wrong or if I took the position that I was right and she was wrong, we would have the makings for a good conflict. Rather than viewing either position as right or wrong, or one being more desirable than the other, we merely recognize that they are positions of difference. And because the difference involves the two of us, adjustment is necessitated.

In attempting to deal with this difference, I could tell Jan to go to social functions by herself . . . but I don't. That would be pretty selfish on my part. Instead, I recognize her need for social interaction and attend these gatherings with her . . . and I do so with a fair amount of joy as opposed to noticeable martyrdom. Jan could expect me to change from being the introvert that I am to become the extrovert which she is. But that would be an unreasonable expectation . . . and one which she does not share. Rather, we accept each other's uniquenesses and make efforts to adjust to them.

Within marriage, we need to accept the fact that there are going to be differences between us and our mates. Recognizing these differences, and then trying to adjust to them in a cooperative fashion, is our goal. By so doing we demonstrate respect for one another and behave in love.

Granted, not every uniqueness of your mate is as easy to accept as this one. In fact, there are some which do not need to be accepted at all. For example, deviant behavior should never be viewed as merely a uniqueness of your mate which ought to be accepted if you really love him.

I met with one client whose husband constantly accused her of being unloving because she refused to accept him as he was. If she were the Christian woman that she claimed to be, she would accept him even though he was different from her. And what was this difference that seemed to present the difficulty? Simply this: he was a drug user. What he called a difference, she called deviant. And she was right.

There are some uniquenesses which are clearly deviant behaviors. A behavior is deviant because it is wrong. Being different is not its problem. Being unacceptable is. But if a behavior is deviant and clearly unacceptable, we must be sure that it is identified as such due to its true nature and not because it is merely different. Different and deviant are not equivalent terms, and a loving mate demonstrates respect by accepting the uniqueness of his spouse.

Acknowledge That Your Mate Has Rights.   All individuals have rights. Being married does not negate this fact. Even though married, I still have the right to my own opinions, beliefs, and feelings, and furthermore, I have the right to express them. But so does my wife. We both have these rights, and few things are more frustrating than the thought that these are being denied us. To deny Jan the right to her opinion, to say that it is of little value, or to simply dismiss it by calmly walking away, is equivalent to asserting that "you don't count" . . . and such a statement is highly disrespectful. I owe her more than that.

As marital partners, we are just that . . . partners. A partnership has been entered with you and your mate both being coequals. There is no place for attitudes of subserviency or supremacy. Both of you have value and are worthy of due respect.

Marriage is not a relationship of denied rights. Oftentimes a mate may choose to relinquish a right. But never should he be denied one. Marriage is a relationship where rights are recognized and appreciated. By so doing . . . by giving respect where it is due . . . we are free to give of ourselves instead of selfishly clinging to what belongs to us.

Honor Your Mate. A final way to demonstrate respect is by honoring your mate. By this I am referring to holding your mate in special regard and letting your actions evidence this fact. Mates need to be treated as though they are special. This is because *they are special*. They have been chosen as a lifelong partner. This choice would not have been made were they not special.

We owe everyone cordiality. But we owe our mates far more. Somehow a husband needs to sense through the actions of his wife that he is honored above all others. Likewise, a wife needs to sense through the actions of her husband that she is his greatest prize. We do this because they deserve it. We do this because it is respectful. And we do this because we behave in love. There is no better reason.

Let me close with two final thoughts in regard to respect in marriage. First, respect is built and maintained by mutuality. In

194

other words, for respect to exist and thrive in your marriage, it has to be *received* as well as *given*. It is totally dependent upon a mutual exchange.

I seriously doubt that respect will continue, whether attitudinally or behaviorally, if you do not find the respectful behavior which you extend to your mate is reciprocated in like fashion. Being considerate, giving, allowing personal responsibility, and all of the other demonstrations of respect become increasingly difficult to continue if the recipient of these acts fails to offer the same forms of respect in return.

It should be noted at this time that, in attempting to behave respectfully, you are in no way giving up the right to expect the same kind of treatment in return. Responsibility in marriage is a two-way street. Both you and your mate have responsibilities and each of you also has the right to legitimate expectations.

Second, a prerequisite to mutuality is self-respect. If a husband has little regard for himself . . . if a wife has only a limited appreciation for her value . . . there is only a poor chance that others will see them any differently. You cannot expect to be respected if you do not respect yourself. Husbands and wives with low self-respect have only minimal expectations regarding how they want to be treated which generally leads to mistreatment. A definite prerequisite to being properly treated by your mate is to expect it . . . and to proclaim it. If you fail to do this, then appropriate treatment, as well as mutuality, is unlikely to occur.

Honesty

Most Christians would be offended by the very suggestion that they behave dishonestly in their marriage. They would recoil with defensive responses like:

"I have never told my wife a lie."

"I have never been unfaithful to my husband."

While it may be true that they have been honest with one another in these obvious manners, the likelihood is quite strong that they have been dishonest in subtle ways.

Be Emotionally Honest.   I had been counseling with Sarah and Matt for approximately four months. As is my fashion, after the first few meetings, the length of time between sessions had increased so that I was only seeing them every second or third week. Over the four months, the relationship had made some significant improvement. This rapid and meaningful turnaround was largely due to the concerted effort of both mates to "pull their marriage together."

I began one particular session with a customary question about how things had been going since our last contact. Both responded with "fine" and took the opportunity to tell me of all of the good things which had occurred. After a few minutes of this type of discussion I began wondering what I was doing still seeing this couple. Maybe it was time to think about termination of the counseling. Still, I was not sure.

I began to question, first to myself, and then out loud, whether things were really as good as they claimed. Finally, I asked Matt to leave the room so that I could spend some individual time with Sarah. As the door shut, Sarah burst into tears. When she had regained composure, she shared with me that there was no comparison to what the relationship had been only four months earlier. Still, although the marriage was in fact greatly improved, there were some aspects of the relationship which continued to trouble her. Sarah then took a few minutes and made me aware of them.

This shed additional light on exactly what was occurring and told me that there was still work to be done. But even greater concern was elicited by Sarah's admitting that she had not made Matt aware of her feelings. Basically, Sarah had been keeping all of her frustrated feelings to herself. Whenever Matt inquired about how she was feeling or whether there were any problems, she would smile and respond, "No, everything is fine." As far as Matt knew, that was exactly the way things were.

Sarah did not view herself as dishonest . . . but she was. She did not think of herself as deceptive or of her actions as being damaging to her marriage. But behavior like Sarah's is extremely dangerous for a relationship. It can have disastrous effects. Sarah was doing what many otherwise honest mates do—failing to be emotionally honest with her mate. When this occurs, a mate is being dishonest.

Although dishonesty of any kind can be extremely detrimental to your relationship, being emotionally dishonest is one of the more damaging forms. You are being emotionally dishonest when you:

- sit on your feelings of frustration instead of expressing them.
- try to appease instead of taking stands.
- express anger in indirect manners such as foot-dragging or other sabotaging behaviors.
- maintain emotional distance by talking only about superficial matters instead of sharing yourself.

These illustrations are not only examples of emotional dishonesty but are also examples of unloving behavior.

Emotional honesty is really a communication issue. Some of us simply have difficulty communicating honestly with one another. When we are being honest, we "talk straight." That is not to say that we "blow others away." There is no place in love for abusiveness, whether verbal or physical in form. But talking straight means that we deal directly with one another. We honestly share what we think and how we feel. In this regard, we speak the truth in love. And this is good.

Deal Directly With Problems. There are other ways in which we lovingly demonstrate honesty within our marriages. One of these is to deal directly with problems. The entirety of chapter 4 was aimed at identifying ways in which we avoid dealing with issues. As I pointed out then, avoidance behavior is never effective. It always leads to negative repercussions. The emphasis here, however, is that in addition to being ineffective, avoidance behavior is also dishonest. To be honest and to behave in love, problems must be dealt with directly instead of being avoided. Failing to bring up a problem, withdrawing from the discussion, or intentionally changing the subject are all examples of marital dishonesty, and dishonest behavior is dangerous for a relationship.

Be Trustworthy. Finally, the more obvious form of honesty cannot be omitted. We demonstrate our love for one another by being trustworthy. Trust is a fragile thing. It can easily be destroyed. Once destroyed, it is often difficult to regain.

Joe and Dana had been married for thirty-five years when they came for counseling. Together, they described their present relationship as a marriage of "ups and downs." Most of their "ups" were related to the amount of time they each invested in their relationship. Their children were now all grown and starting families of their own. This left Joe and Dana plenty of opportunities to spend time together. They had a group of friends with whom they were quite socially active. Besides just social events, they did many other things as a couple, such as tennis, traveling, and gardening. As they took time to invest in their marriage in these ways, they found a great deal of enjoyment together. These were the "ups."

Whereas the "ups" occurred as a result of a number of activities, their "downs" were always precipitated by a single event . . . an event in the past. Joe was a salesman and had to do some limited traveling. On a business trip, after twenty years of marriage, Joe had a one-night fling with an associate's wife. Dana was made aware of the situation by an irate husband. Their marriage faced a severe crisis at that point and, to the outside observer, it appeared as though the couple emerged with their relationship intact. Unfortunately, the ghost of that one indiscretion kept haunting them.

Joe's employment still requires that he travel. Even though he is away from home with far less regularity now, his absence continues to prompt anxiety in Dana.

The marriage was good fifteen years ago. In fact, due to the fighting we have been going through since Joe's "fling," it was probably in better shape then than it is now. If he would step out on me then, what's to stop him from doing it now. Maybe he's been doing it all along. How do I know he hasn't?

Joe strongly denied any other women in his life either before the event of fifteen years ago or since. But he also pointed out, in much exasperation, that his denials did little good. Dana seemed to be able to block the incident from her mind for periods of time. During these periods when her memory was in remission, things between them went fairly well. But whenever the event of fifteen years ago reasserted itself, conflict emerged. Trust is a precious commodity. It needs to be guarded. A momentary lie, careless action, a single indiscretion . . . any of these is capable of bringing long-lasting consequences. For Joe, fifteen years of honest living had failed to restore things to the way they once were.

Joe's indiscretion was an obvious form of untrustworthiness. There is no difficulty in recognizing the dishonesty evidenced by his action. A far less obvious variation of the violation of trust, yet still disastrous for a relationship, is described by this statement: "He'll use it against me."

I most frequently hear this as a complaint from mates who claim that their marital partners do not fight fair. What they are saying is that, when they do share their feelings and thoughts, they usually end up finding them thrown back at them at a later time . . . and in a twisted fashion. After a few such experiences, they stop sharing. Their trust is destroyed. Without trust in a relationship, superficial interaction is used to maintain a safe distance. And with superficiality and safe distances, a relationship dies.

Honesty is a characteristic of behaving in love. For the Christian, whether it is:

- sharing his true self with his mate (being emotionally honest);
- dealing directly with problems; or
- being trustworthy,

it is a responsibility. But even more than that, it is the bedrock upon which a relationship is built.

Forgiveness

There are many biblical instances where the issue of forgiveness is dealt with. Whenever this is done, the conclusions are unmistakably the same: Christians are a forgiving people. It is a differentiating factor. It distinguishes Christians from the world. As a critical Christian characteristic, forgiveness is not optional equipment . . . it is standard. When wronged by an individual in a given situation, a Christian forgives.

Our difficulty with forgiveness does not rest with the clarity upon which the command is given. We hear the command and we want to obey. Rather, we are troubled with some aspects of application. The troublesome questions which I most frequently encounter seem to emphasize one of two themes: (1) the number of participants required in the act of forgiveness or (2) repetitive occurrences of the same behavior. Both of these themes have particular significance within the special relationship of marriage.

1. The number of participants required in the act of forgiveness.
Is forgiveness an act which requires two willing participants? Does someone have to ask for forgiveness before it can be granted? Are you supposed to forgive someone even if they do not ask for it? Is there a particular advantage to having two participants involved in the act of forgiveness . . . a "forgiver" and "forgivee"?

When it comes to determining just how many people have to be involved with forgiveness, our example is clear. It only takes *one* willing participant for forgiveness to occur.

"Father, forgive them; they do not know what they are doing."

Luke 23:34

These words of Jesus leave little doubt as to the answers to our questions. Our responsibility is clear: We forgive. "But he hasn't admitted to anything!" We forgive. "But she refuses to say that she is sorry!" We forgive. "But he hasn't asked for forgiveness!" We forgive. But, but, but, . . . this could be an endless dialogue. But the Christian's response is always the same . . . forgive.

The number of participants required for forgiveness to take place, therefore, is clear: It only requires one. However, when the question changes to "How many people are required for a relationship to be restored?", our answer changes. Behaving in a forgiving manner does not necessarily mean that the relationship will be restored. For restoration of a marriage to take place, a couple must first be reconciled to one another and reconciliation requires the willing participation of *both* mates . . . not just one.

Jesus' description of the prodigal son provides us with a clear example of what is required for reconciliation to take place. The son wanted his share of inheritance. His father gave it to him. The son then immediately embarked on a journey to a distant country where he squandered his money on reckless living. This life-style was totally contradictory to the values he had been raised with. After living in this manner for a while, and being subjected to many hardships as a consequence of his behavior, he "came to himself." In essence, he recognized the error of his ways. It was then that he decided to return to his father's home and ask his forgiveness. I will pick up the remainder of the story with Luke's account:

> "I will set off and go to my father, and say to him, 'Father, I have sinned, against God and against you; I am no longer fit to be called your son; treat me as one of your paid servants.' So he set out for his father's house. But while he was still a long way off his father saw him, and his heart went out to him. He ran to meet him, flung his arms around him, and kissed him. The son said,

'Father, I have sinned, against God and against you; I am no longer fit to be called your son.' But the father said to his servants, 'Quick! Fetch a robe, my best one, and put it on him; put a ring on his finger and shoes on his feet. Bring the fatted calf and kill it, and let us have a feast to celebrate the day. For this son of mine was dead and has come back to life. He was lost and is found.' "

Luke 15:18–24

The relationship between the father and the son was reconciled. But what allowed this to occur was not the father's willingness to forgive alone. Nor was it the son's genuine remorse and request for forgiveness alone. Reconciliation was possible because both of these aspects were present. There was a genuine "forgiver" . . . and there was a genuine "forgivee." With reconciliation achieved, healing in the relationship could begin.

Within a marriage, the restorative potential which emanates from the act of forgiveness is totally based on mutuality. Just as in the example of the prodigal son, it is sought, granted, and received . . . oftentimes with both mates being in turn "forgivers" and "forgivees." Whether it is one mate who has done the wrong or both, reconciliation comes with conjoint effort.

When the forgiveness process is not entered with mutuality, emotional distance remains between the mates. Intimacy is blocked and each mate begins to feel estranged. Even though a mate has been forgiven, the closeness that existed between the marital partners is interrupted. Repeated occurrences of this type of incident—forgiveness but no reconciliation—continually broaden the gulf into relational deterioration.

Forgiveness is a command. We are supposed to do it but its effectiveness is truly limited by the number of willing participants. Granting forgiveness when it is not sought, forgiving a mate for misdeeds even when denied, or forgiving a mate who seeks it only because he has been "caught" is what we are supposed to do. It is the responsible action of a Christian mate. If one mate chooses to behave irresponsibly, it does not relieve the other of the expectation to behave in a responsible manner but the effectiveness of the forgiveness experience is greatly limited. For the restorative potential found within this healing action to be realized, the process must be entered into with mutuality.

2. *Repetitive occurrences of the same behavior.* What about cyclical patterns? Do you keep on forgiving the same misdeeds even when they repetitively keep occurring? Does this type of forgiveness help or hurt? When is enough truly enough?

Most people find forgiveness to be a far less confusing issue when the indiscretion in question is an isolated incident as opposed to a repetitive behavior. Infrequent rudeness, occasional outbursts of anger, seldom encountered insensitivities . . . there is little question as to what needs to be done in situations like these. With the repeat offenders, however, such as the husband who physically abuses his wife and then remorsefully asks for her forgiveness; the wife who can't help herself when it comes to overextending the credit accounts; the husband who can't seem to keep his hands off other women; the wife who continually lapses into periods of drunkenness, our clarity diminishes.

Is there a point where a Christian wife says: "Enough is enough; I cannot forgive you anymore for your actions!"? Does a husband's automatic forgiveness for a wife's indiscretions merely contribute to the cyclical nature of the repetitive behavior?

In order to dispel the confusion which exists around the problem of repetitive misbehavior, there must be a distinction made between (1) our willingness to forgive and (2) our willingness to be continually damaged by the repetitive misbehavior of an irresponsible mate. The first of these is an obligation—the second is not.

Our willingness to forgive even in repetitive situations is clearly commanded by Jesus. As I indicated in chapter eight, when Peter came to Jesus asking how often he had to forgive his brother who continued to wrong him, Jesus' response of "seventy times seven" was not an attempt to extend the limits but to eliminate them (Matthew 18:22). From Jesus' perspective, it made no difference whether this was the first offense or the one-hundred-and-first. The response is still the same . . . forgive.

Even though the obligation to forgive is clearly noted, however, this does not mean that a continually offended mate is in any way prohibited from taking some responsible measure to insure self-protection. Simply stated, forgiveness is not license. It was never intended to be a process which allowed the continuation of irresponsible behavior.

Forgiveness is extended in the *present*, for an occurrence of the *past*, but in no way precludes expectations for the *future*.

Do not think, if you are busy forgiving your mate, that you do not have the right to expect responsible behavior. Forgiveness does not create license for your mate to act as he pleases. It does not exempt your mate from responsible behavior. Forgiveness is not intended to allow unacceptable actions to be maintained or for disruptive marriages to continue unchanged. Quite the contrary, forgiveness is intended to offer troubled marriages the possibility of healing.

Through forgiveness, an otherwise chaotic relationship can progress in a restored condition. Reconciliation, restoration, healing, growth . . . these are the intent of the forgiveness act. To manipulate it for any other purpose is to render it ineffective. But unfortunately, this is very frequently the case where repetitive misbehaviors are concerned.

Changing the cyclical nature of repetitive misbehaviors requires drastic measures. At some point in time, the offended mate has to take a stand. This decision is then followed with a statement to this effect: "I will no longer tolerate this irresponsible behavior."

Taking such a stand and making such a statement means different things for different people. For some it is saying, "I will no longer be responsible for the consequences of your misbehavior. You will have to solve your own problems." This means the faithful wife will no longer bail her rowdy husband out of jail and the compassionate husband will no longer make excuses to friends and employers for his wife's drunk behavior. In the first case, there will be no more rescuing. In the second, there will be no more protecting.

For some couples, taking a stand may involve an even stronger statement and more decisive actions.

Jim and Theresa had been married seventeen years. Throughout the marriage, Jim repeatedly abused Theresa physically. "I don't know why I do it. I just get mad and can't help myself. I love my wife and it hurts me to hurt her." He was always remorseful . . . always sorry . . . and always forgiven. After the ninth trip to an emergency room, Theresa finally took a stand.

Frank and Sharon had been married ten years. While Frank had endeavored to be faithful to Sharon, she had had five affairs (that he knew about). Sharon always came back to Frank and said that he was the one she really loved. She didn't know why it was so difficult for her to remain true to him. After Frank became aware of affair number six, he took a stand.

Tom and Rita had only been married for three years. During that time, Tom had had fourteen jobs. His longest length of employment at any job was four weeks and it was not uncommon for him to leave after only a few days. There was always "a problem" with the job. He ran up bills and refused to pay them. Rita went to work in order to provide basic necessities but found Tom uncooperative when it came to helping with child care. When she became pregnant with their second child, she took a stand.

Mike and Becky had been married twenty years. Gradually, Becky had become more and more dependent on the pills she was receiving from her long list of physicians. Although she did not drink, her inability to function in public and at home resembled what Mike understood to be the symptoms of alcoholism. Finally, Mike took a stand.

All four of these offended mates came to the same conclusion concerning their marital relationship:

> I can forgive my mate for his/her irresponsible behavior, but I can no longer continue to live with this reoccurring disruption. For my own sanity, I must remove myself from this situation until I have an indication that things will really be different.

When mates choose to try to stop the cyclical nature of repetitive misbehavior by withdrawing from the situation or becoming maritally separated, I strongly encourage the establishment of some clear-cut criteria to be met for reconciliation to be considered. The goal here is for the desired change to be identified in specific and measurable terms. In the case of Jim and Theresa, it would be reasonable to expect Jim to enter some form of professional treatment and for any contact between the two of them during the separation to be absent of violence. For Frank and Sharon, reasonable expectations would include professional treatment and demonstrated exclusivity in regard to her sexual behavior. With Tom and Rita, a period of gainful employment would be a minimal prerequisite. And finally, Mike would probably expect Becky to be involved in professional treatment and to abstain from the use of any addictive substances which could affect her in the same manner as did her pills.

The theme of this line of reasoning is one of requiring the repeat offender to prove that a change has occurred rather than either (1) promising a change or (2) merely assuming that no change is really required. Forgiveness is not an automatic approval for misbehavior to be continued.

Precedent for this line of reasoning was established by Paul when he cautioned Timothy to "not be over-hasty" in restoring an offender within the Church (see 1 Timothy 5:22). Was the offender forgiven? Absolutely. Was he accepted back into the fellowship? Surely. But was he placed back into positions of responsibility? Probably not. At least, not until he had had an opportunity to prove that he was truly a changed person and one who was ready for new responsibilities. I believe the same attitude can be very justifiably applied to marriage.

The expectation of responsible behavior in a mate is *not* non-Christian. We are to forgive. Doing so is a demonstration of behaving in love. Yet, our forgiving attitude should never be interpreted as license nor lead to cyclical patterns of irresponsibility. To forgive, and then take a stand, is sometimes the most difficult demonstration of love a mate can show.

Commitment

A final characteristic of behaving in love is commitment. This is a familiar term to those in Christian circles and is ordinarily associated with spiritual decisions. I only infrequently hear the term commitment used in regard to marriage. At those times, it is usually mentioned in the context of one of two situations . . . both negative. For the sake of simplicity, I will refer to these as Situation A and Situation B.

Situation A.   I usually observe Situation A within the domain of my counseling practice. A classic example would be David and Judy, who came to my office in the midst of a marital crisis. Judy had recently announced her intention to divorce David. With a fair degree of calmness, she described sixteen years of marital discord. The relationship hit a snag on the honeymoon and had continued its decline ever since. David was selfish, demanding, and totally insensitive to her needs.

> I have no say within the marriage at all. David totally discounts me. He takes no responsibility for providing for my financial needs and seems to be disinterested in the children as well. I have had enough.

And what was David's response to Judy's assessment of their marriage? In short, he was in total agreement.

> You're right. I've been all that you say I've been. But I can change. I know you've asked me to change many times before and I've always ignored you. But things are different now. The vows I took when we married are important to me. I swore before God that I would take you "for better or for worse." I made a commitment for life. I thought you did, too. If you divorce me, you are violating the oath you took before God.

For sixteen years, David had been irresponsible while Judy had been responsible. For sixteen years, he had taken while she had given. For sixteen years, he had discounted her very existence while she struggled to maintain some degree of self-esteem. Now, after all of this, David was accusing Judy of violating her commitment to stay in the marriage.

Situation B. Unlike the preceding example, Situation B is seldom seen in counseling. I usually witness this more as an outside observer or as a friend and confidant. A good example of this situation would be Mark and Kathy, who had been married for more than twenty years. They had one son in college and two in high school. To the outside observer, there was little to suggest that they had anything but a normal marriage. But within the confines of the home, the facade was removed and emotional tension abounded.

At a church retreat, Mark began to reveal to me the private pain he was experiencing. It had been years since he and Kathy had said anything kind to one another. Although the two of them didn't argue as much now as they did in the earlier days of the marriage, Mark figured that he and Kathy had just learned to stay out of each other's way. Kathy kept busy by involving herself in the lives of the children. In a similar fashion, Mark overinvested in his career. Neither Mark nor Kathy was happy. In fact, they were both fairly miserable. Yet they cooperatively maintained the relationship. Together, they kept the marriage intact.

I asked Mark exactly what kept him and Kathy together:

> Neither Kathy nor I believe in divorce. We both vowed to stay married as long as either of us should live. Neither one of us wants to violate that vow. We are committed to the marriage. I guess we'll just continue to live with things as they are.

For over twenty years, Mark and Kathy had lived together in misery. Neither Mark nor Kathy liked the relationship as it was but they didn't know what to do. Being committed to the marriage, they were willing to let things drift along as they were.

Both of these examples demonstrate erroneous perceptions of what commitment in marriage is actually supposed to be. In Situation A, commitment is a *tool* to be used. David is obviously trying to manipulate Judy. He is exerting control over her by using the fact that she had made a commitment to the marriage. His years of irresponsibility are of little consequence. With fervor and determination, he uses the fact that she had made a commitment much like a blacksmith uses a hammer. Judy is pounded with her commitment in an attempt to force her to remain in the marriage.

In Situation B, commitment is used as an *excuse*. Both Mark and Kathy use the fact that they had made a lifelong commitment to the marriage as a justification for apathy. They are legitimizing their misery and probably feel a little saintly because of their martyrdom. Of course, the idea of working on the relationship in an effort to improve it is never seriously considered. They don't have to do that. Their commitment was to the institution of marriage . . . not to the relationship.

It is interesting to note that, in both of these situations, all that can be remembered of the marital ceremony is that a commitment was made to remain in the marriage "so long as you both shall live." I would hate to think that this one remembrance is all that remains from such a significant occasion. The minister in situations like these is cast more as a judge in the act of sentencing than he is a facilitator for entering a blessed union. In reality, the commitment made between mates extends far beyond this erroneous perception.

Having suggested what commitment is not, it is time to suggest what commitment is. Webster's dictionary defines commitment in the following way:

- an agreement or pledge to do something in the future;
- something pledged.

As is suggested in this definition, whenever a commitment is given, it obligates the person making the pledge for something in the future. By its very nature, then, commitment is not a solitary act. It always involves consequential actions. For example, I may borrow my son's tape recorder and promise to return it in a day. Although the act of commitment is enacted when I borrow the recorder, it will not be completed until a time in the future when the item is returned.

This explanation seems simple and straightforward. However, things get a little more complicated when we look at commitments made within the context of relationships. Frequently, this type of commitment takes on an added dimension. Whereas the commitment made to my son would be met by a single act at some specific time in the future, relational commitments often take on an ongoing nature. For example, friendships are often based on a commitment of honesty. Friends expect honest behavior from friends. This is an expectation which cannot be met by only a single act in the future. A one-time occurrence will not suffice for such a relational commitment. Rather, this form of commitment must be practiced continually.

Repeatedly, consistently, continually . . . friends fulfill their commitment to be honest. Similarly, within marriage, the truly significant commitments are typically of a relational nature. The obligations are not met with a one-time payoff. Instead, they are constantly being fulfilled.

When our attention is directed specifically toward marriage, I think it is important to examine exactly what commitment is being made. What are mates committing themselves to do when they enter marriage? Even in a time when the writing of personal vows is fashionable, most ceremonies contain the same vows which have been pledged between mates for decades. In one derivation or another, mates typically make the following commitment to one another:

"Will you love, comfort, honor, cherish, keep (in sickness and in health), forsake all others, so long as you both shall live?"

First of all, I think it is interesting to note that the marriage ceremony actually contains a *number* of pledges as opposed to only one. There are pledges to love, to comfort, to honor, etc. But more importantly, if not *most* importantly, it should be recognized that the pledges taken at the time we enter into marriage fall into two separate and distinct groupings. Collectively, the pledges found in these two distinct groups form two basic commitments. There is a commitment made to marriage as an *institution* . . . and there is a commitment made to marriage as a *relationship*.

Marriage as an institution.   Marriage as an institution is expressed in the wedding ceremony by the traditional phrase "so long as you both shall live." Such a commitment establishes the time frame in which marriage is to function. Simply stated, marriage is forever.

Making such a commitment is extremely important to marriage. More than simply establishing a time frame, commitment to marriage as an institution also allows a number of vital elements to emerge. It is really an act which initiates a process which will unfold within the context of "forever." A commitment of "forever" establishes security and endurance, as well as the potential for marital growth. Without these elements, a marriage is equivalent to the proverbial house built on sand.

Ken and Joan had been married less than a year when they came for counseling. Both identified "communication difficulties" as their marital problem. As I began to explore what this meant, they both gave me instances where they simply could not reach an agreement. None of these issues appeared extraordinarily major. But that wasn't too unusual. The problems in marriages are seldom "the issues" anyway. About midway through the session, and much to my surprise, Ken suddenly blurted out, "I don't know if I can stay in this marriage. If Joan doesn't stop complaining about things, I may get out. I can't take the hassle."

My surprise came from the seemingly inappropriateness of the statement within the counseling context. I wasn't exerting any undue pressure on Ken. Joan hadn't just attacked him. Things actually appeared quite calm. Then what had happened? As it turned out, Ken was merely stating his perspective of relationships in general and his lack of commitment to marriage as an institution. "If it isn't going to be hassle-free, I'm getting out."

How do you think a statement and attitude like this affected Joan? This is what she had to say:

Ken has said the same thing at home a number of times since we got married. That's really why we're here now. It hurts me to think that he could get out of this marriage so easily. It makes me mad and sometimes causes me to wonder why I am trying so hard. I feel as though I might as well give up.

He usually says this when I'm complaining about something that isn't going well between us. When he starts talking about getting out of the marriage, I get scared and back off. I try not to upset him. It's like walking around on eggshells. I can't say anything that may be construed as confrontative because Ken sees that as hassling. We never get anything resolved.

Making a commitment to marriage as an institution is not meant to be a sentencing. Its intent is to offer security and stability. All couples have conflicts. Every marriage has to make adjustments. Feeling secure in a mate's commitment to the marriage allows the opportunity for dealing with conflicts and for needed adjustments to occur. This is what makes marriage resilient.

A marriage can endure many affronts, whether from within or without, if the commitment to marriage as an institution is strong. It takes this kind of commitment for growth to occur. Ken and Joan are an example of what happens when the commitment is absent. There is no security. Joan feels no freedom to be herself or to be honest. She must appease and avoid. Without a commitment to marriage as an institution, the relationship between Ken and Joan will not grow. In fact, it will only continue to weaken.

Marriage as a relationship.   Commitment to marriage as a relationship is expressed in the wedding ceremony by every vow except "so long as you both shall live." Vows to love, comfort, honor, cherish, keep, and to forsake all others . . . all of these collectively form a commitment to marriage as a relationship. They state what one mate will do for the other, as well as what is expected to be reciprocated.

The commitment to marriage as a relationship allows for the development of intimacy. Within the secure context established by the institution of marriage, the relational vows are fulfilled. By plan and design, mates can give to and receive from one another demonstrations of love. By so doing, they foster growth and closeness in all of the dimensions of love. At least, this is the ideal.

Things do not always go according to plan, and not infrequently, there is no plan at all. Hectic schedules, selfish motives, the demands of daily living . . . these culprits and many like them combine to dim our memory of exactly what was said during the wedding ceremony. The once spoken vows are forgotten. The once-demonstrated pledges of love become absent behaviors.

Commitment to marriage as a relationship is essential to marital stability and embodies the emotional quality of the marriage. It contains the feelings level . . . the "want to" . . . the desire which keeps mates directed toward one another. It allows for internal strength as opposed to external coercion. In other words, if the relational aspect of a marriage is high, mates stay together because they want to and not because they have to.

When my daughter was seven years old, she told me about a game she and some of her friends had played. It was called "wedding." She was the minister, two of the children were the prospective mates, and the remainder of the group were attendants. I asked her how the game was played.

> Well, I had Jimmy and Missy stand in front of me and all
> the other children line up beside them. Then I started the

ceremony. I said: "Jimmy, do you take Missy to be your *awfully* wedded wife?"

Needless to say, my wife and I have had chuckles over her version of the marriage ceremony. Sadly though, the behavior demonstrated by some mates suggests that their vows may have been more in line with this slip of the tongue than with the more traditional variation. For relational quality to be high, mates have to place their commitment to marriage as a relationship in a priority position. Neither the fulfillment of the pledges nor the potentially positive consequences will simply *just* happen. They both occur through premeditated effort.

Commitment is a characteristic of behaving in love. When Christians marry, they make commitments to both marriage as an institution and marriage as a relationship. To neglect either one of these is to violate the commitment to marriage. To emphasize marriage as an institution to the exclusion of marriage as a relationship is to participate in legalism. Its product is a dry shell which maintains itself through external coercion. To emphasize marriage as a relationship to the exclusion of marriage as an institution is to be guilty of irresponsible laissez-fairism. Its product is an unstable relationship totally at the mercy of the prevailing emotional wind.

A prerequisite to marital stability and growth is a commitment to both marriage as an institution and marriage as a relationship. Commitment to marriage as an institution establishes a context in which growth can occur. Commitment to marriage as a relationship guarantees that the act by which a marriage is built will be demonstrated. Together, and only together, a marriage is made.

Final Thoughts

Marital failure is a process—not an act. It is a destination which is journeyed toward—not an initial port of entry. And like most

215

journeys, the process of marital failure requires both time and the taking of many steps. Step by step . . . one irresponsible action followed by another . . . slowly but surely . . . the destination is approached.

Irresponsible behavior, whether through acts of omission or commission, is the culprit of marital failure. Being in love while not behaving in love is the Christian variation of this malady. For the Christian, behaving in love is a responsibility. But more than that, it is the practical implication of a Christian's faith.

The Apostle Paul seems to bring things down to a practical level. I think this was his aim when he tried to define love for the Corinthians. Although he was not speaking directly of the marital relationship, his perceptions are worthy of notice.

> Love is patient; love is kind and envies no one. Love is never boastful, nor conceited, nor rude; never selfish, not quick to take offence. Love keeps no score of wrongs; does not gloat over other men's sins, but delights in the truth. There is nothing love cannot face; there is no limit to its faith, its hope, and its endurance.
>
> 1 Corinthians 13:4–7

I do not know how totally loving we can ever be. Whether it be with our respect, honesty, forgiveness, commitment . . . there will be times when the demonstration of our love will be deficient. Yet, at least we have a direction in which to proceed and goals toward which to strive. Christians are to "love one another." For mates, this responsibility has an even greater significance encompassing both being in love and behaving in love.

— 11 —
ESTEEMING
YOUR
MATE

Kay and Wayne had a failing marriage, although not exactly a drifting relationship. While Wayne comfortably pursued outside interests, Kay *un*comfortably waited for his attentions to be directed toward her. Fortunately, events prompted them to seek counsel before the failing nature of their marriage had progressed to a point of disaster.

With counseling, Kay and Wayne made significant progress in their marital relationship. Although most of my time was spent with both of them together, some intervention was addressed to Kay alone. This is a fairly common practice of mine when dealing with the particular problem which plagued their marriage. When trying to interrupt this particular marital scenario, I typically attempt to get the uncomfortably waiting mate to focus on things of personal interest such as friendships, groups, school, time alone, athletic endeavors, etc . . . "What do you want to do for yourself?"

Although my intervention with this couple had progressed well in most areas, the entire line of thinking ("What do you want to do for yourself?") seemed to stall. Kay resisted most of my suggestions and encouragements. Whether directly or indirectly, she simply failed to make any changes in her life. Finally, in an emotion-laden individual session, Kay began to sob. She then proceeded to inform me of some of her difficulty:

I don't know what I want to do for myself. I don't even know who I am anymore. I used to. When we married, Wayne and I both worked. I felt confident, competent, valued, and received a lot of positive strokes at work and home. What I had to say counted for something because I contributed to the income.

Then came the children. When I decided to quit my job and stay at home with the children, things began to change. All of a sudden, I was less important. What I had to say no longer counted as much as it once did. If I wanted to do something that would require a little adjustment and cooperation on Wayne's part, I would get a response something like this: "You expect me to come home early from work and take care of the kids so you can go out? It's too difficult to work that into my schedule." Wayne even told me that he didn't want me to get a baby-sitter. The message which I began to hear through all of this was, "You don't count." My self-esteem really took a nose dive. I don't know who I am anymore or what I want. I feel worthless.

Kay's experience is not an unusual one. Although the specifics can vary considerably from couple to couple, the theme of being gradually discounted is one which I frequently hear.

I have found an interesting phenomenon to occur when a mate is repeatedly told, "You don't count." Whether the message is through the medium of words or by actions, the recipient of the message gradually begins to believe it. And as the message takes its toll on the individual, it also takes its toll on the marriage. With most of the couples seen in my counseling practice, either one or both of the mates complain that their spouse does not really care about them. They feel unvalued, undesired, and often, unloved. As a marital nonperson, they simply do not count.

Feeling uncared for and believing oneself to be of little value to a mate creates a myriad of responses, none of which is good for the relationship. If allowed to persist, the discounting of a mate, and the repercussions which come from it, can wreak havoc upon a marriage. The discounting of a mate, however, is not only counterproductive to the development of a healthy marriage, it is also contradictory to Scripture. Paul makes this explicitly clear in his first letter to the Christians in Thessalonica. He was concerned that the "brethren" continue to be supportive of one another. The King James Version of Paul's advice is as follows:

> Comfort yourselves together and edify one another.
>
> Thessalonians 5:11

The New English Bible states it like this:

> Hearten one another and fortify one another.

Comfort, edify, hearten, fortify . . . regardless of the translation, Paul's intent is clear. From his perspective, a Christian's responsibility is to *encourage* and *build up* . . . not to *discourage* and *tear down*. If this is a Christian's responsibility toward a brother or sister in the Lord, how much more of a responsibility is it toward a mate?

Do we really think Paul's admonition is important? Do we really need to be all that concerned about encouraging our mates? Do we have to build them up? I believe we do. In fact, I believe this area to be of such vital importance to the enhancement of a marriage that I rank it as the second greatest marital responsibility which a Christian has to accomplish. In a very real sense, living with a mate ought to make him or her a better person. I wonder how many of us could actually claim this to be the case in our own marriages.

Comfort, edify, hearten, fortify, encourage, build up . . . trying to address all of these terms becomes a cumbersome task. I prefer to summarize this entire concept into one theme . . . *esteeming*. This single term seems to embody in a concise manner all of the other elements to which Paul refers. The remainder of this chapter will identify exactly how you go about accomplishing the task of esteeming your mate.

The Practice of Esteeming

Dealing with a topic like esteeming your mate can prompt some initial confusion. For example, we may ask ourselves, "What exactly is 'esteeming'?" "How is it actually done?" In order to clear up some of the confusion which may be present, I want to differentiate between the more *behavioral* demonstrations of esteeming and those with an *interpersonal* bent.

Behavioral demonstrations of valuing or esteeming are the simple acts of caring. They are the tangible behaviors referred to by Dr. Richard Stuart in his book *Helping Couples Change*. He frequently asks couples to develop "Caring Days Lists," which consist of positive acts of caring that are easily accomplished. Some examples include: a demonstration of affection (hug, pat, kiss, etc.); a card or note; a flower; a night out without children; and an unsolicited compliment. Tangible, visible and easily accomplished, these are the behavioral demonstrations of caring and esteeming.

As essential as these acts are to the nurturing of a healthy marriage, their presence does not always denote esteeming. At times, they truly are performed from a stance of genuine concern. At other times, however, they represent a more perfunctory or even calculating attitude. If you will recall the chart regarding Sensitivity/Insensitivity in marriage (chapter 5), the sensitive category actually contained three separate variations. Each variation was distinguishable by motivation and intent. The same can be said of these behavioral demonstrations. Sometimes the performance of these esteeming behaviors more accurately reflect an attitude of "If I were to act *as if* I cared, I would . . ." instead of the true and genuine expression of valuing a mate.

Responsibly, a wife is given a hug.

Routinely, a husband is given a card.

Manipulatively, a wife is taken out to dinner.

Calculatingly, a husband is complimented.

Positive acts, nongenuinely given, are *not* examples of esteeming.

Genuinely offered behavioral demonstrations of esteeming are good. They need to occur frequently. Yet, as essential as they may be to the growth and nurturing of a healthy marriage, they are not the most important form of esteeming.

The bedrock of esteeming within marriage actually lies in the interpersonal realm. More than the mere execution of an act, interpersonal forms of esteeming demand greater personal and emotional investment from a mate. The focus is more upon an ongoing relational interaction as opposed to the committal of a single act. Less tangible; requiring greater effort; far less susceptible to other than genuine motivation; significantly more powerful as an influence for good upon a marriage . . . the characteristics which distinguish this form of esteeming from its behavioral counterpart are clear and concise. In a further effort of clarification, however, I have chosen to highlight five specific ways in which mates can esteem one another interpersonally.

Being a Good Listener

Suggesting that there is a "good" anything automatically indicates that there is also a "bad." This dichotomy is no more profoundly evidenced than in the area of listening. Being a good listener is not an easy task. It requires deliberate effort. But the failure to exert the effort can have detrimental effects on a marriage. Being a poor listener sends the message, "You don't count." In short, we listen to those whom we value. When it comes to listening, there are two primary characteristics which help to distinguish between those mates who do a good job and those who do not.

A good listener is an active listener.   A husband who is an active listener gives more than an occasional nod or a strategic "uh hmm." He gives his attention. Intense, unpreoccupied, and undivided, his attention is directly offered to his wife. No sorting through the mail. No scanning through the newspaper. No looking past his wife in order to keep up with a plot of a television program. These adjunctive tendencies are resisted. Rather, he deliberately involves himself in the conversation.

He responds to what is being said. He listens. He summarizes. He asks questions. He clarifies. He makes personal observations. He does all of these things because he is actively involved in the conversation. What is being said, and the person saying it, are both important to him. And this importance is conveyed by his active participation.

A good listener is a responsible listener.   A responsible listener is one who recognizes that his role will frequently vary. Sometimes he will be expected to offer suggestions and solutions to problems. "I'm not sure what I should do. What do you think?" At times like these, an examination of the possible options, potential consequences of each, and a personal opinion of what might be the best solution are quite acceptable. At other times, however, a mate may be expected to act only as a sounding board. Rather than offering solutions, he listens and responds in a manner which allows his wife to solve her own problem. It is not always an easy task to determine which of these two roles is expected . . . or needed. Some of us are prone to be answer givers. Others of us are prone to refrain from ever making committal observations. Either tendency, if allowed in an unbridled fashion to predetermine our response style, can interfere with the process of listening.

A responsible listener will ask himself the following question:

What does my mate want from me . . . suggestions or a sounding board? After answering this question, an appropriate response is given. This offers the best opportunity for meeting your mate's needs.

Sharing Yourself With Your Mate

We *share* ourselves with those whom we value . . . we *withhold* ourselves from those whom we do not.

Sharing yourself with a mate is a definite form of esteeming. To behave in this manner clearly makes the statements: "I think you are important" and "I care about you." For this concept to be applicable to our lives, it is imperative that we gain a practical understanding of what is meant by sharing, especially within the context of a marriage.

The term *sharing* carries with it the connotation of giving. Mates who share within a marriage give of themselves to their mates. When used in the theme of esteeming, I see two primary ways in which this is done. Both of these are a good measure of the true value which one mate has for another.

Giving your time.   One form of sharing involves the amount of time which you give to your mate. This is really a *quantitative* issue. It is easily measurable. Whether in increments of seconds, minutes, hours, days, weeks, or months, the time given to one another can be calculated. With this summation, the value of your mate is often determined.

- How much time do you give to your mate?
- Who or what gets more of your time?
- Of the things which compete for your time, where does your mate fall on the list of priorities?
- In the midst of a hectic life, how much effort is exerted in order to make time to be together?
- Who usually initiates this kind of action?
- What is the real importance of time together?

Questions like these help to assess our present situation. Due to the statements of valuing which are made by the giving of our time, it is important that an evaluation of this nature be done fairly regularly. Time is one of our most precious commodities. How it is invested can have a far-reaching effect on both your mate and your marriage.

Giving yourself. The second form of sharing is really a qualitative issue. It deals with what actually takes place during the time which is spent together. Sitting together in front of the T.V., taking an afternoon to go sailing, spending a weekend at a resort but failing to converse about anything other than superficial matters . . . although much needed respites for many of our lives, these are examples of *relaxing*—not *relating*. And as such, they are not quality times. A qualitative sharing, or the giving of yourself, is encompassed by the willingness to be self-disclosing. The very process of self-disclosure implies trust, confidence, and genuine concern for your mate. Whether your mate is sharing himself or, in reverse, is actually inviting you to share with him, esteeming is taking place.

In an effort to stay in touch with his wife, a friend of mind would spontaneously ask the question, "What's going on in your world?" He would do this at times which would allow for an appropriate response. This seemed to work well for them. They were able to dodge the tendencies of mundane relaxation and deal in depth with where each other really was. Some of us, however, may need a little more planning to accomplish self-disclosure. Regardless of the form it may take in our respective marriages, the sharing of self is a clear indication of valuing and, thusly, a definite act of esteeming.

Viewing the Concerns and Interests of Your Mate as Important

Mates are different. No matter how many similarities which may exist between the partners in a marriage, there will always be dissimilarities. Frequently, these differences are in the area of personal interests.

Personal interests are not generally great moral issues. Intrinsic qualities of right and wrong or good and bad are notably absent. Rather, personal interests tend to be simply matters of preference. Whereas you may prefer one thing, your mate may prefer something else. An example with which I am most familiar would be my own marriage. Jan is an artistically talented individual. I am not. Being a creative person, she has tried her hand at about everything imaginable. At one time during our married life, she was particularly interested in English smocking, a form of fine needlework. The unique elegance of the smocked designs enabled Jan to make distinctive clothing for our children.

Jan began by taking a class and then quickly progressed to the self-taught method. Soon, she was teaching classes of her own and creating original smocking designs. A friend approached her about going into business for themselves. In a short time there was "Smock-A-Memory," a dual-owned company which created and produced smocking designs for sale throughout the United States.

The smocking story continued, but the point I want to make involves the interest and response of a husband (myself) to all that went on during this smocking adventure.

My basic response was one of interest, support, and encouragement. Through my wife's excitement I was exposed to the different types of stitches, basic design differences in patterns, pros and cons of various kinds of floss and fabric, etc. I could thread and operate a pleater and occasionally soloed as a parent while Jan went to weekend craft shows and clothing markets in Atlanta. In essence, because of her interest, I also became involved in smocking.

Now, although I can probably tell you a great deal about smocking, it is unlikely that I will ever take it up as a personal hobby. In and of itself, it never held a personal attraction for me. However, my personal disinterest in smocking never caused me to view it as unimportant. The overriding factor was the fact that it was of interest to my wife. Jan *is* important to me. So the things which are significant to her are also significant to me.

It is a self-centered personality which measures importance only through the eyes of his own personal interest. Being supportive of an endeavor which may not be of personal interest, solely because it is important to the one you love, is a way of esteeming your mate. It denotes that you care.

Affirming Your Mate

Another means of esteeming mates is through the affirmation of who they are. Affirmation, or the act of affirming, is best understood by first recognizing what it is not. Affirmation is not rejective. Mates are not affirmed by telling them what they are doing wrong. Neither is affirmation corrective. Mates are not affirmed by telling them what they "ought to," "should," or "must" do right. Within affirmation, there is no place for the negative. To the contrary, there is only room for the positive.

To connotatively describe affirmation, we have to use words like *validate* and *confirm*. There is the sense of saying to a mate, "You're okay. In fact, you're better than okay. You're fine just the way you are." In affirmation, a mate is accepted for *who* he is, *what* he is, and *as* he is. It is an act of building up as opposed to running down.

It is unrealistic to think that a mate has only positive characteristics . . . that he only does good things and makes pleasant statements. We are all too well aware that this does not accurately reflect the real world. Even the best of us have chinks in our armor. Even though we would prefer to live in a world comprised of only the positive, there are times when a mate's behavior not only warrants criticism, but requires it. It is at times like these that we offer statements which are corrective in nature.

But with the recognition that marriage encompasses both the good and the bad comes a further realization that the negatives should never be the primary focus in a relationship. Negatives should never be our predominant preoccupation. Unfortunately for many marriages, however, this "shouldn't" accurately describes the manner in which mates relate.

"The squeaky wheel gets the grease" did not become an old adage through infrequent occurrence. It is vivid evidence of our tendency to focus on the bad as opposed to the good. Minuses seem to far more readily capture our attention than do pluses. Problems, difficulties, squeaky wheels . . . although a part of reality, are still not the focus of affirmation. For the affirmation of a mate to occur, three steps are required.

Understanding. In order to be affirming, you must first truly know your mate. Far beyond mere acquaintanceship, there has to be a recognition of his basic character. What is his motivation? What is his intent? What does he believe? What does he value? As you can see, understanding goes far beyond simply watching what he does. True understanding—recognizing your mate for what he is—transcends the superficial. It is depthful. And it is essential.

Appreciation. The second step of affirmation is the appreciation of what you discovered in step one. Very frequently, our difficulty with appreciation is most noted in the area of "differences."

"I like one thing and my wife likes another."

"I am this way and she is another."

"I do it this way and she does it another."

In short, differences create problems. In order to be affirming, we need to change how we view some of these differences. Rather than seeing our mates as totally negative because they are different, we must instead view them as unique and special.

Many of the differences between mates can be viewed as positive as opposed to negative. Frequently, these perceived differences are actually complementary. An example of this complementary aspect would be the social differences which exist within my own marriage. As I shared with you earlier, Jan tends to be extroverted whereas I tend to be more introverted. In essence, we balance each other out. Rather than being problematic, our differences in this area work hand-in-hand to help bring balance to our marriage. Importantly, I appreciate Jan's difference . . . and she appreciates mine.

Whether differences are an issue or not, there must be an honest appreciation felt for the unique characteristics of your mate. Without this appreciation, affirmation will not be achieved.

Acknowledgement. The final step in affirmation is the act of communication. In one way or another, the appreciation which is felt toward your mate must be expressed. Sometimes this is done verbally.

"I like the way you look . . . feel . . . smell."

"I like the way you respond toward the children . . . me . . . others."

"I think you're a caring person."

"I appreciate you.

Statements like these are clear examples of verbal affirmation. But there are many other ways also. Helping out with your mate's responsibilities, making special plans for just the two of you, being supportive of something which is important to him . . . all of these are expressions of affirmation. They all communicate that your mate is valued for who he is. And they all help build him up.

Affirming a mate—focusing on the positive and accepting him for what he is—frees him to be more of what he can be. It is a definite act of esteeming. As such, it builds both your mate and your marriage.

Valuing Your Mate's Opinion

A final means of esteeming is demonstrated by the willingness to accept a mate's opinion.

- What does your wife think about a given situation?
- How does your husband feel about your options?
- What opinion does your mate have regarding what you should do?

Sometimes the situation is of such a nature that it only concerns yourself. At other times, it is a problem which pertains to both you and your mate. Regardless of whether the problem is yours alone or both of yours together, the value which is placed on the opinion of your mate communicates a clear message . . . either for good or for bad.

Valuing your mate's opinion does not mean that the observations and suggestions which are offered have to be followed. There should be no strings attached. Especially with those problems which are clearly yours alone, it is you who are still ultimately responsible for making the final decision. The problems are your problems. The choices are your choices. And the consequences of your decisions are your consequences.

Opinions should be freely given . . . and freely received. As such, your mate's opinions should be considered as valuable data. They are to be used in your decision-making process. And when this is done, even though there is not the guarantee of blanket endorsement, there is the implication that your mate's opinions are both meaningful and significant to you. In reality, this is, in and of itself, highly important.

The opinions of your mate come in two separate contexts: (1) solicited and (2) unsolicited. Of the two, solicited opinions are probably the easiest for you to accept. They are typically invited and desired. In one way or another, you seek out the perspective of your mate.

"What do you think about this?"

"How do you feel about that?"

"What do you see my options to be?"

"What should I do?"

By requesting an opinion, you are generally far more prepared to receive it. On the other hand, you may not be as prepared to receive opinions of an unsolicited nature. A defensive response, an unwillingness to discuss, a refusal to acknowledge another perspective . . . these are but a few of the reactions sometimes prompted by unsolicited opinions. Without a doubt, uninvited opinions are potentially more difficult for you to deal with. Still, whether solicited or not, how these opinions are handled has a significant impact on your marriage.

Lee and Alice came for counseling after twenty-five years of marriage. Unlike some couples who can remember good times in the earlier years followed by a gradual decline in their relationship, Lee and Alice only had memories of bickering. In effect, they were well-seasoned adversaries. They had argued for a quarter of a century. Finally, weary of the warfare, they were seeking help to either change the marriage or end it.

As is common with this type of relationship, both mates were accusational:

"He wants to dominate me and has always done as he chooses."

"She is nonsupportive and resists any decision I may make."

As counseling proceeded, it became clear that there was some truth to what each was saying. For twenty-five years, their only efforts of cooperation had been at being uncooperative. Even though their respective roles were easily identifiable, both agreed that Alice's part in the scenario seemed to be more of a learned defense. She did not enter the marriage planning to resist Lee's decisions. But when she found her opinions falling on deaf ears, her self-esteem began to decline. It was then that she determined to make things miserable for Lee.

> I don't think he's ever cared about what I've thought or felt regarding anything. The few times that he did listen to my suggestions didn't make any difference. He just went on and did what he wanted. How do you think that made me feel? I decided that if he wasn't going to pay any attention to me, I wasn't going to pay any attention to him. He may make the decisions, but I could make life miserable.

Twenty-five years of this kind of combat—Lee pulling and Alice dragging her feet—had left many scars. Each was bitter and resistant to change. How much better things would have been if Lee had only valued Alice's opinions.

Many things are communicated through the willingness to value your mate's opinions. The first message which is communicated is: "I have confidence in your judgment." Obviously, you would pay little attention to someone in whom you had no faith. Contrarily, you pay a great deal of attention to someone in whom you have confidence—and the expression of confidence is something which your mate will find extremely reassuring. The second message which is communicated is: "You count." You are taking into consideration how your mate thinks and feels. You do this not just because of your confidence in his judgment, but because he is important to you. You **want** to. In that you care, his observations are significant. A final message which is communicated is: "The entire world does not revolve around me." Rather than totally "watching out for number one," there is the shedding of a self-centered attitude as you try to see the situation from the perspective of others. In an effort toward being understanding, you ask the question, "How do you see it?" and then you respond to the answer given.

The messages that were described in the preceding paragraph are all esteeming in nature:

"I have confidence in your judgment."

"You count."

"The entire world does not revolve around me."

These help build up your mate. All that is required in order to send messages like these is for you to value the opinion of the one you have married. When you think about it, that does not seem to be a terribly demanding task.

I have just highlighted five specific ways in which mates can esteem one another interpersonally. How did you fare? If you were to rate yourself as an esteemer, would your grade be an "A"? Would it be a "B"? Or do you deserve something more toward the failing end of the scale?

Regardless of how you are doing now, there is always room for improvement. Fortunately, with concerted attention, improvement is always achievable.

- Being a good listener.
- Sharing yourself with your mate.
- Viewing the concerns and interests of your mate as important.
- Affirming your mate.
- Valuing your mate's opinion.

None of these is an impossible task and regardless of the effort required, the benefits will always surpass any personal investment you may make.

The Benefits of Loving and Esteeming

The focus of the last two chapters has been on the identification and clarification of the two primary responsibilities of Christian mates. As indicated at the outset, I approached the subject of responsibilities with some degree of hesitancy. The mere mention of the word tends to invoke numerous unpleasant feelings. We are not particularly fond of "oughts" and "shoulds."

Still, at least within the context of Christian marriage, I do not believe the unpleasant feelings and the sighs of resignation often associated with doing what we "should" are necessarily warranted. It really depends on how we choose to view the whole issue of responsibility. If we choose to view marital responsibilities as unwarranted demands and infringements upon our individuality, we will find ourselves constantly "kicking against the pricks." However, if we view them as helps and guides to aid us in our quest of a fulfilling marriage, we will joyfully embrace them. I personally view them within this latter context. Responsibilities are positive and not negative. Loving and esteeming are responsibilities but, as with all other divine directives, they are meant for our benefit.

God's directives are always purposeful. They are never given arbitrarily and it is always beneficial to follow them. The most obvious benefit of adhering to the biblical admonitions for mates to love and esteem one another is in the area of the *quality* of the relationship. Loving and esteeming constantly lead a couple to greater levels of intimacy and marital satisfaction. We marry for intimacy and closeness, and that part of us which truly needs to love and be loved is fulfilled in a vibrant and growing marriage. Following God's directives allows this to occur. Through being responsible mates, we attain that which we desire.

In addition to the enhanced quality of the relationship, loving and esteeming also produce the benefit of marital resiliency. In reality, this ability to withstand the natural stresses which assail married life is actually an added benefit. It is a by-product of the increased marital satisfaction which we just discussed.

It's really quite simple to understand. Happy marriages are stronger marriages. When mates are satisfied with the relationship, they are far more willing to do what needs to be done. The "want to" is present. It is always easier to do what you are supposed to do when you truly feel like doing it. The greater the degree of pleasure and satisfaction being experienced within a marriage, the greater the willingness to do what needs to be done and, consequently, the greater the resiliency to potential disruptive forces.

Peter recognized this added benefit of love nearly two thousand years ago in his first epistle:

> Above all, keep your love for one another at full strength, because love cancels innumerable sins.

> 1 Peter 4:8

Keeping our love *for* one another at "full strength" makes getting along *with* one another an easier task. And within marriages, love being at "full strength" is essential.

There are no ideal marriages and there are no ideal mates. We all have chinks in our armor and we all are prone to error. Unintentionally, humanly, mistakenly . . . no matter how hard we try to do things right, there will be times when we do them wrong. How a marriage fares during these crucial times of stress often depends on the level of love which exists between mates. Forgiveness, sensitivity, honesty, respect, speaking the truth in love . . . these and all of the other constructive exchanges which need to take place within a marriage are more easily extended when love is at "full strength." Love truly does cancel innumerable sins.

I do not know how completely loving and esteeming we can ever be. Whether it be with our giving and forgiving or our listening and affirming . . . there will be times when the demonstrations of our love and the esteeming of our mates will be difficult. The hecticness of life, the counterproductive interactional patterns, the personal and individual quirks which make us unique (but, at times, also difficult to live with) . . . these are but a few of the many things which can inadvertently interfere with our doing what we ought to do. Yet, we at least have directions in which to proceed and goals toward which to strive. As we assess the vast benefits to be gained, there is no question as to whether the journey is worth the effort.

— 12 —
COUNSELING: WHY, WHEN, AND WHO?

Having spent eleven chapters discussing the drifting marital scenario, as well as the factors which contribute to marital success and failure, I do not feel as though this book would be complete without addressing the issue of counseling. Even though not all marriages will need counseling, a divorce rate of approximately 50 percent coupled with the realization that some couples who remain married will do so unhappily, makes it apparent that many marriages could benefit from professional intervention.

When I first began to write this chapter, I sat for a while in my study trying to imagine some of the questions that might confront a couple as they contemplated the possibility of marital counseling. Here are some of the questions I came up with:

"Should we go for marriage counseling?"

"Maybe we should wait. I mean, are things really that bad?"

"What will my mate think about it? What if he/she refuses to go?"

"Who should we see? How will we know if we're seeing the right person?"

"Will it really help?"

"What will it cost?"

Although there are many more, I believe that most other questions would only be variations of these.

When it comes to trying to decide whether or not counseling should be sought, troublesome questions are the norm and not the exception. It seems to make little difference as to the degree of difficulty being experienced within the relationship. Whether only mildly dissatisfied or totally exasperated, the same questions seem to occur. The fact that these questions are normal, however, has little effect on the ease in which they are answered. They are still difficult. Each couple must evaluate their own relationship; each must determine their own personal need; and each must ultimately make their own decision. By providing clarifying information, the making of that decision can possibly be an easier task. This chapter has been written with that goal in mind.

Why Should Counseling Be Sought?

Just as there are both right and wrong reasons for choosing to marry, there are also right and wrong reasons for choosing to seek marriage counseling. Before discussing the right reasons, it will be helpful to identify the wrong ones.

The Wrong Reasons

Justification. One wrong reason for seeking marriage counseling is justification. Some couples simply want to be able to claim that they have tried everything possible in an attempt to resolve their marital difficulties. If they can claim to have "even tried counseling" (to no avail), they feel more justified in either calling it quits or continuing in their self-destructive patterns.

My personal record for encountering this particular wrong reason for seeking counseling was established by a couple who had their first (and only) counseling session with me at 11:00 A.M. one Tuesday morning. Shortly after the outset of the session, they informed me of their 1:00 P.M. court appointment. In only two hours, their divorce was supposed to be finalized.

Although this particular couple is an extreme example, they accurately represent those who seek counseling for justification. They had little intention of working on their marriage. However, they, too, can claim to have "tried counseling."

Conspiracy. Another wrong reason for seeking marriage counseling is conspiracy. It is similar to leaving a baby in a basket on the doorstep of an unsuspecting family. Take for example the Greens. Mr. Green wants out of the marriage . . . Mrs. Green does not. Mr. Green feels guilty about totally abandoning his wife, so he conspires to leave her on the doorstep of an unsuspecting counselor. Under the guise of seeking professional help for the marriage, Mr. Green agrees to attend counseling. Once contact is made, Mr. Green feels free to leave the marriage. His wife's emotional adjustment is now the responsibility of the counselor.

Coalition. A final wrong reason for seeking marriage counseling is coalition. In this errant maneuver, one or both mates are more interested in finding someone who will listen to their complaints regarding their spouse than they are in any improvement in the relationship. They assume that any reasonable counselor will readily see just how rotten their mate is. It is thought that, once the counselor comes to this realization, he will undoubtedly form a supportive coalition against the culprit. Obviously, just like justification and conspiracy, coalition also offers poor motivation for counseling.

The Right Reason

If justification, conspiracy, and coalition are examples of wrong reasons for seeking counseling, what are the right reasons? Actually, there is only one good reason for seeking counseling: *You want your marriage to be better than it is.*

Some of you may be thinking: "Surely, every couple who wants a better marriage does not have to go to counseling." I would agree with this statement. Every couple probably does not have to go. But for those who:

1. are dissatisfied with the relationship in its present condition;
2. seem powerless to create any constructive change on their own; and
3. are willing to work at making things better,

marriage counseling is a good option.

The three criteria listed above are ideal. Their presence can make the job of a marriage counselor an easier task. In reality, however, counselors are often forced to work with far less. It is usually the exception for us to see two cooperative mates, both of whom are ready and eager to work on their marriage.

Some mates come to counseling reluctantly. They're not sure if this is what they want to do. Others feel coerced into coming. Tired of the struggle, they finally give into a persistent mate. Lastly, still others come in a confused condition. They're not even certain about what they truly want to see happen in their relationship. But even with these less-than-ideal circumstances, however, improvement can still be noted.

Deterrents to Counseling

Some of the more common deterrents that prevent couples from seeking counseling are:

Failure to recognize the need. If you are not aware of a problem, it is difficult to do anything about it. I find the failure to recognize the need, however, to be usually an issue of degree. Even though some clients report in astonishment: "I never realized that there was even a problem"; what they really mean is that they did not realize the problem had gotten as bad as it apparently had.

Although marital failure frequently gains access in subtle forms, few of these scenarios emerge totally without notice. There is usually some recognition of difficulty . . . some hint of dissatisfaction. This recognition, however, is apparently not significant enough to catch anyone's *full* attention. Instead, they continue on . . . as if everything is fine. They continue, that is, until a crisis rocks the marriage. Then they seek help.

Fear. A far more obvious reason for failing to seek counseling is fear. This particular deterrent has a number of variations. There is the fear of stigma; "What will others think? We have an image to maintain." There is also the fear of failure; "What if counseling doesn't help our situation?" Finally, there is the fear of admission; "If we admit that there is a problem, we will have to deal with it. We will no longer be able to pretend with one another that everything is okay."

Fear is a great deterrent. It acts on a marriage much like paralysis does on the body: It impedes movement. What seems to aid in breaking the paralysis is asking the question, "What do I have to lose? Even if what I fear does take place, will I really be any worse off than I am now?" In reality, there is little to lose. This realization can lessen the deterring grip which fear can have on a marriage.

The real travesty with these deterrents is that they delay the taking of any constructive action. They cause time to work against us. If left unattended for any reason, troublesome relationships will only continue to be troublesome. Problematic marriages seldom get better on their own. They only continue to deteriorate. So the greater the length of time that the marriage is allowed to continue without attention, the greater the deterioration.

If you and your mate have both recognized a need for change

and, after personal effort, you have failed to achieve it, counseling is a good option to pursue. To continue to delay will only work against your marriage.

When Should Counseling Be Sought?

Not long ago I asked this very question of a group of married college students. They were completing a semester's worth of study in the area of "Understanding and Enriching Your Marriage." Since they were now well informed, I was certain that they would all give me good answers. With this anticipation, I was a little surprised with the response of one of the older students:

> I probably would not go until things had deteriorated to the point of seeking divorce. In other words, until it was too late.

Although his answer was not exactly what I wanted to hear, his candid and honest response came closer to representing reality than did the other "good" answers.

There are two points of interest noted in this student's response. The first is his suggestion that a marriage can deteriorate to the point of no return . . . to a time when it is too late to turn things around. This is really a complex and difficult issue to address. Theoretically, it can be argued that marriages never reach the point of absolute no return. Especially with Christian marriages, there is always hope. Mates can change and healing can take place. Although this makes sense, we do not live in theory . . . we live in practice. And in practical living, many couples seem to reach a point in their relationship where they believe things will never get better and at this point, they often divorce.

Marital deterioration is not an instantaneous point *in* time . . . it is a process *requiring* time . . . and lots of it. Marital failure does not occur overnight. It is painstakingly nurtured by years of neglect, disinterest, and/or avoidance. If a couple makes a decision that, at least for them, any chance of revitalization within the marriage is too late, it is a decision that is reached only after many missed opportunities for change.

The second point of interest noted in my student's response was the time at which he indicated counseling would be sought. He would not seek counseling until "things had deteriorated to the point of seeking a divorce." Although his response was consistent with what I have observed as a counselor, it is not what I typically hear people say. None of my other students were so inclined in their responses. They all reported that counseling would be sought much earlier in the cycle of marital deterioration.

After giving this some thought, I believe that what we are really talking about here is the difference between what we think we would do and what we actually end up doing. The combined responses of my other students are not really surprising. I think that it is only human nature to give ourselves the benefit of the doubt. We naturally tend to see ourselves doing the best thing far more frequently than we actually do it.

To explore the difference between how people believe they would behave and what I actually witness them doing, I designed a questionnaire and distributed it to a number of church congregations. Among other things, they were asked at what point they believed that they would seek counseling for their own marriage. They were given choices which gradually moved from a lesser point of marital deterioration to a greater. Here is the question as it appeared on the questionnaire:

If there were problems within your marriage, at what point would you seek counseling? (Place an X by your first choice.)

_____ When demands from outside of the marriage begin infring-
ing upon the relationship.

_____ When you are unhappy with the emotional quality of the relationship (feeling little love from/for your mate).

_____ When your mate becomes increasingly insensitive to your needs.

_____ When there are specific problems which you cannot work out on your own (i.e., sexual, financial, division of labor, etc.)

_____ When you begin failing to resolve disagreements more frequently.

_____ When your frequency of arguing increases.

_____ When the two of you stop talking/communicating.

_____ When you first consider the possibility of getting a divorce.

_____ When something potentially disastrous to the marriage occurs (i.e., an affair).

_____ When a decision has been made by one of you to either separate or divorce.

_____ Never.

Somehow, their responses were not surprising to me. With few exceptions, the overwhelming tendency was to select answers toward the top of the list. In other words, they believed that they would seek counseling early in the process of marital difficulty. Although an admirable response, it was largely inconsistent with my experience as a counselor.

I do not think those who answered this question were intentionally trying to falsify their responses. Rather, they were simply giving themselves the benefit of the doubt. It is easier to give right answers than it is to do right behaviors. The couples whom I see in counseling tend to be at the bottom end of the list. Consistent with the response given by my one student, they are much further along in the process of marital deterioration.

All of this strongly suggests that counseling needs to be sought early. Look at the list of points of marital digression identified in my questionnaire. Dealing with marriages which are concerned with external demands, early emotional dissatisfaction, or the first signs of insensitivity (top of the list) are far easier tasks than dealing with relationships encountering total communication disruption or imminent divorce (bottom of the list).

When it comes to seeking counseling, the higher up the list a couple is, the better. Do not let the marriage deteriorate to the bottom of the list before seeking help. This strategy only increases the possibility of things becoming too late.

Who Should Be Sought to Counsel?

A simple and obvious response to this question is "someone who is qualified to help." A far more difficult task comes with defining what is meant by the word "qualified." Being Christian only adds more difficulty to the couple's task. It becomes another variable which must be reckoned with as a selection is made. Finding a qualified marriage counselor is not an easy task.

According to my survey, the overwhelming majority of respondents would seek help from either their pastor or a professional Christian counselor. Here is the question which I asked:

If you wanted counseling for your marriage, from whom would you seek help? (Place an X by your first choice.)

_____ A friend

_____ Your pastor

_____ A pastor (not yours)

_____ A Christian counselor (professional)

_____ A non-Christian counselor (professional)

This response seems to be consistent with most research literature. In conservative Christendom, there is a tendency to shy away from strictly secular professionals. The reason for this is based on a broad range of fears commonly held by conservative Christians. There is the fear that spiritual concerns will be ignored or, even worse, that they will be viewed as pathological. There is also the fear that secular counselors will ask them to do things which violate their moral standards. Fears of being misunderstood, misdiagnosed, and/or misdirected underlie most of a conservative Christian's mistrust for the secular world.

For the Christian couple seeking qualified marital counsel, there are two primary areas which must be considered: (1) counseling preparation and (2) spiritual perspective.

Counseling Preparation

Those who counsel should be adequately prepared to do so. Many are . . . but some are not. All counselors are not alike. In evaluating the appropriateness of an individual's preparation to counsel with marital difficulties, the following three questions should be asked:

Question #1 What has been your formal preparation for counseling? Your concern here is with the level and kind of formal academic preparation which the counselor has received. I have a brief synopsis of the major categories of individuals with formal preparation to counsel. They are ranked here in a descending order of cost, rather than competence.

A *psychiatrist* is a medical doctor. His specialization is in the treatment of individuals with severe emotional problems as opposed to relational difficulties. Some psychiatrists do pursue additional training in relational areas, but a psychiatrist is not the counselor of choice if the problem within the marriage is not the result of severe emotional difficulties being experienced by one of the mates.

A *clinical psychologist* is trained in individual behavior and assessment. Although qualified to provide testing and individual counseling for personal problems, psychologists are not typically well versed in relationship counseling. Unless specialized training in relationships has been pursued, a psychologist is not the counselor of choice.

Unlike psychiatrists and psychologists, *marriage and family counselors* are not always well governed by state licensing requirements. Although a marriage and family counselor is supposedly a specialist in relationship counseling (thus becoming a likely candidate for working with marital problems), the degree of training can vary broadly. In fact, in some states, very little training is required at all for someone to consider himself a qualified marriage and family counselor.

In states where no license is required, it is important to inquire as to formal academic degrees and the nature of the training. Furthermore, most qualified counselors are affiliated with a national professional organization. For marriage and family counseling, this is usually the American Association of Marriage and Family Therapy. A counselor should be able to readily answer any questions regarding training or professional affiliation.

Social workers were historically found in agencies which provide various forms of human services. Today they are often found in counseling roles, although their particular training may or may not have prepared them for this. Like the others who have been described, it would be best to ask a few specific questions regarding the amount of training in counseling that was received, especially in the area of marital relationships, before a decision is made to counsel with a social worker.

A number of clergymen refer to themselves as *pastoral counselors*. Although there are seminaries which prepare and graduate individuals with formal degrees in pastoral counseling, not all of those who claim the title possess the degree. Sometimes, pastors who find themselves doing a lot of counseling adopt the title because it matches what they do.

Like the other categories previously described, a couple seeking qualified help needs to be willing to ask questions. Inquiring about graduate degrees which have been awarded and the particular area of specialization studied (individual problems, spiritual problems, marital and family problems, etc.) will help determine whether the pastoral counselor is a suitable alternative.

While on the subject of formal preparation, there are various academic degrees that are earned. The *bachelor's* is the first significant degree awarded by a college or university and requires approximately four years of full-time work. Although a bachelor's degree can be received in some specific fields of human behavior (psychology, social work, behavioral science, etc.), it is not recognized as adequate training to offer oneself as a professional counselor. Instead, it is viewed as a prerequisite degree to doing further formal training. When this further training is obtained at a college or university, it is called graduate work.

The next degree is the *master's*. It requires an additional 1½–2 years of full-time graduate work. The master's degree is the generally accepted minimum standard for counselor readiness. A master's degree is available in many professional fields.

The final step in the academic ladder is the *doctoral* degree. It requires several years of full-time work after the master's degree has been achieved. Those who hold a doctorate, regardless of their area of specialization, are called "Doctor." Those who *do* not *are* not. Again, there are many different doctoral degree programs. For example, not everyone holding a doctorate is a psychologist. There are doctorates available in marriage and family therapy, as well as many other counseling areas. *Be sure to ask.* Professionals are always prepared to explain their credentials.

Question #2 What specialized training do you have in dealing with marital problems? Not all counselors are alike. Those who are well qualified to deal with some problems are poorly qualified to deal with others. Psychiatrists, psychologists, social workers, and pastoral counselors are not routinely prepared to deal with marital difficulties. Yet, there are some psychiatrists, psychologists, social workers, and pastoral counselors who are excellent marriage counselors. Marital counseling is their area of expertise. When this is the case, it is either because their formal training was uniquely different from that usually received by professionals in their category or they have taken the initiative to receive additional training. In either case, a counselor who claims to be an expert in marital counseling should be able to substantiate his assertion.

Question #3 How many years have you been counseling troubled marriages?   Another important factor in determining the suitability of a marital counselor is the degree of experience he has had. Generally speaking, the longer a counselor has practiced his profession, the more proficient he is in his field. We do learn a great deal from our experiences, and for counselors, long years of working with couples can greatly enrich the quality of intervention.

All counselors begin somewhere. No one begins with a great deal of experience. However, counselors with lesser experience are frequently under the supervision of a professional with greater experience. If the counselor being considered is fairly new at intervening in marital conflict, regardless of his formal preparation, it may be good to inquire whether he is being supervised by a more experienced professional. If not, an alternative choice may be advisable.

Spiritual Perspective

For Christians, a counselor's spiritual perspective is extremely important. It is interesting to note that, with conservative Christians, issues of spirituality tend to exceed even concerns for professional counselor preparation. In my survey, I addressed this issue with the following question:

What qualifications would you desire this person (whom you have elected to counsel you) to have? (List 4 in order of importance.)

(1)_____

(2)_____

(3)_____

(4)_____

As you can well imagine, I received a wide variety of responses. Some respondents even went so far as to identify a preferred age and sex of the counselor. Yet, with rare exception, the requirement that the counselor possess a similar Christian perspective was always toward the top of the list. It was plain that Christians wanted to be counseled by other Christians. Some went so far as to require the counselor to be of the same denomination.

This spiritual aspect of counseling was very important for most of the respondents. In fact, it was not uncommon to find spiritual criteria addressed and professional training to be totally omitted. Sometimes, the professional characteristics received at best only token acknowledgement (have a degree; some knowledge about marriage; have some training in counseling). My personal opinion is that a healthy balance between professional and spiritual qualities needs to be reached. I do not want to discount the importance of the spiritual dimension, but I believe that the emphasis of spiritual qualities to the exclusion of professional training is a grave error. To eliminate the spiritual in favor of the professional could be as grave an error.

Counselees, whether Christian or not, work best with counselors who possess similar value systems. Understanding, trust, and comfort are far more easily achieved when this commonality exists. But even more importantly for the Christian is the need to be counseled by someone who guides not just through the understanding of human relationships, but also through the awareness of the spiritual dimension of our humanity. For the Christian, spirituality is a way of life . . . and it is an area which must be dealt with during the counseling process.

Pastors as Counselors

I cannot leave the question of "Who should be sought to counsel?" without addressing the issue of pastors as counselors. Being a Christian professional, I have worked a great deal with pastors over the past number of years and can make three observations:

1. Counseling goes with the territory, but is not generally desired. Most pastors counsel. Some do it often. Few enjoy it. Rather, it is typically seen as a part of their pastoral role—it goes with the job. Pastors do not enter the ministry to counsel. To the contrary, a priority list showing what they believe to be their responsibilities would always have counseling somewhere down from the top. Still it is a responsibility and, as such, one which is dutifully performed.

2. Marriage counseling often interferes with opportunities to minister to a couple. This seems to be a contradictory statement. Some see counseling and ministry as synonymous occurrences and in some ways they are. Yet in other ways they are different. Blending the roles of pastor and marriage counselor is a most difficult task to accomplish.

To effectively intervene as a marriage counselor frequently requires confrontational behavior. Furthermore, a great deal of personal information is related in marital sessions. Sometimes these two factors combine to hinder a pastor's ability to minister to a couple in a spiritual dimension. In essence, his primary responsibility is then negated.

3. Generally speaking, pastors are not adequately trained to counsel. Pastors are not exempt from the training requirements utilized in determining who is qualified to counsel. Some pastors like to counsel and are adequately prepared through graduate education or specialized training programs. However, if formal preparation is absent, other alternatives should be considered.

In closing, determining who should provide marital counsel is not always an easy task. For the Christian couple, however, the selection of a suitable helper should not be determined solely on spiritual values any more than it should on professional preparation. A solution based on either of these criteria alone will only increase the possibility of counselor ineffectiveness. A more appropriate choice would be an individual who possesses *both* of these essential attributes. Whether the choice be a pastor or a Christian professional, spiritual depth and professional skill are both prerequisites to sound intervention.

Is Marriage Counseling a Process Which Requires the Participation of Both Mates?

Does marriage counseling take place if only one of the mates is present? Can there be improvement from counseling if one mate is absent from the process?

I believe that marriage counseling is an attitude more than it is a behavior. As such, it is far less reliant upon composition than it is upon the skill and goals of the counselor. Following this stream of thought, having two mates present is no more of a guarantee that marriage counseling is actually taking place than the absence of a mate is ruling it out. Much depends upon the focus and intent of the counselor. If his interventions are aimed at changing the interactional patterns of the relationship, then marriage counseling is taking place regardless of who is present or absent during the counseling session. Seeing only one mate is not the ideal and can create another set of problems with which a counselor must deal. But improvement in a marriage can be attained through counseling only one interested partner.

The question of whether marriage counseling can be conducted with only one mate carries with it an implication which needs to be addressed. What is the attitude of the absent mate? Is it one of "I do not choose to go to counseling but I don't care if you go" or is it "I do not choose to go to counseling and I don't want you to go either"?

Obviously, the latter statement is the one which creates the greatest degree of difficulty. Deciding to seek marital counseling against the wishes of a mate is seldom an easy decision. Yet, even with one disapproving mate, my tendency is to suggest that the partner who is concerned about the welfare of the marriage at least accept responsibility for himself and seek help.

Encouraging Signs

Marriage counseling is not a panacea. It is no cure-all. As a solution for troubled relationships, it is no more perfect than the marriages which it attempts to help. Still, it seems to be about the best alternative which we are presently able to offer.

Within Christendom, there are signs of encouragement which seem to suggest that the future may be even more promising for counselor intervention. One such sign of encouragement is the growing acceptance of a change in attitude. The myth that "Truly Christian marriages do not need counseling" is being replaced with a far more realistic perspective which acknowledges that Christians are not exempt from problems. Whether they be circumstantial (i.e., "it rains on the just and the unjust"; see Matthew 5:45), personal (i.e., depression), or relational (i.e., marriage and family difficulties), Christians, too, will have their fair share. Salvation does not make an individual an instantaneous "clone of Jesus." A Christian has a great deal of humanness, and being human, is susceptible to the things which interfere with living a perfect life.

Another encouraging sign is the growing acceptance of Christian professionals. Once seen as suspect (as though Christian and professional were contradictory terms), there seems to be an increasing appreciation for the blending of spiritual insights and the understanding of human behavior. The flip side of the same coin is the increasing expectation by those Christians who are seeking help that their counselor not only be spiritually compatible, but professionally sound as well.

Both of these changes are encouraging. Things are looking up. Hopefully, the greater acceptance of our susceptibility to problems will foster the earlier detection of marital difficulties and, subsequently, earlier intervention. With the concertive effort being made toward integrating faith and clinical practice, the possibility of improved counselor preparation is increasing. The future does appear to be promising for Christian marriage counseling.

CONCLUSIONS

The Future of Christian Marriage

There is a part of me which thinks that "conclusions" should be your task as a reader and not mine as a writer. Yet my more responsible self realizes that this is more accurately a shared responsibility. I need to state mine and you must determine yours.

In glancing back over the past twelve chapters, it seems that there is ample information upon which to derive some conclusions. From the outset I identified how intimacy, though greatly desired, often eludes us; how the failure to grow toward intimacy frequently launches marriages into the drifting scenario of marital failure; and how the contributors to this failure are multiple as opposed to singular. I also addressed the subject of Christian responsibility and the characteristics which aid in the prevention of drifting. It would not be difficult to draw conclusions which could be prefaced with words like *ought* or *should*: "Being Christian, I ought to do this"; "You should do that."

There is, throughout this book, the potential for many conclusions. Maybe this is where we should share our responsibility. You can formulate conclusions regarding what enables or prevents marriages from growing. You can decide how Christian mates ought to behave toward one another and how they should not. You can decide what priority marriage should have for a couple and how this priority is to be maintained. And you can conclude which of the contributors to marital failure seems to give you the most personal difficulty. You have read the material and need to determine these conclusions for yourself.

But if this is your task, what is mine? While you wrestle with multiple conclusions, I will restrict my comments to the singular. While you draw conclusions *about* the content, I want to project *from* it.

We live in a chaotic time. Changing social values, political intrigue, military powers, superpowers, and instability all seem to be the order of the day as opposed to the exception. Still, even in the midst of chaos, I believe the future of Christian marriage is good. If being Christian gives us anything, it is the reality of hope and the realization that *God always has a future for His people*:

- For the newlywed couple, riding high on enthusiasm and optimistic expectations, *God has a future*.
- For the 20-year veterans with a vibrant and healthy marriage, *God has a future*.
- For the drifting couple who suddenly becomes aware of the distance which has crept into their relationship, *God has a future*.
- For the couple in crisis, *God has a future*.
- And even for the one who has been left to stand alone by a mate who decided that things were too late, *God has a future*.

Regardless of where we are in the sequence of marital life, *God has a future for us*.

I do not think that we always make the best choices in life. In fact, some of our choices are pretty poor. Sometimes our erroneous decisions are intentional. We know what we should do, but we do something else anyway. But mostly, our poor choices are less malignant. We want to do the best thing but, caught up in the feelings of the moment, the future consequences of our choices are dimmed and the result is pain.

Although some of us manage to make poor choices more

consistently than others, no one is exempt. We all have regrets. None of us *always* makes the best decision. Still, regardless of the choices of the past and the circumstances of the present, *God always has a future for us*. We can change what is happening if we will just turn control of our lives over to Him and take responsibility for that which He gives back.

Depending upon the choices we have made, God's future for us may not be what He would have planned earlier in our lives. Our decisions may have added a few twists, turns, and detours, and these departures from His plan may now necessitate greater adjustment and effort on our part. For the Christian, the future of marriage is always potentially good. It all depends on whether we are ready to deal with our marriages responsibly. All that remains is to make the commitment.

Still, *God has a future for us*, and a future with God is always good.